BEE COUNTY COLLEGE
ATE DUE

25609

KF
9660
.Z9
I5

Inbau

Evidence law for t

D1071021

BEE COUNTY COLLEGE

You have accepted the responsibility of either
returning this book when due or paying the $1 a week
penalty.   NO overdue notice will be mailed to you.
The college business office will notify you if money
is owed the college.   This book can be renewed for
one week either in person or by phone (358-7032). A
book returned by 10 a.m. on the third overdue day will
not be charged a fine.

COLLEGE

EVIDENCE LAW
FOR
THE POLICE

Inbau Law Enforcement Series

KF 9660.29 I5

EVIDENCE LAW
FOR
THE POLICE

FRED E. INBAU
Professor of Law, Northwestern University

MARVIN E. ASPEN
Judge, Circuit Court of Cook County, Illinois

FRANK CARRINGTON
Executive Director, Americans for Effective Law
Enforcement, Inc., and former Police Legal
Advisor, Denver Police Department

CHILTON BOOK COMPANY
PHILADELPHIA   NEW YORK   LONDON

LIBRARY
BEE COUNTY
COLLEGE

25609

Copyright © 1972 by
Fred E. Inbau, Marvin E. Aspen and Frank Carrington
First Edition   *All Rights Reserved*
Published in Philadelphia by Chilton Book Company
and simultaneously in Ontario, Canada,
by Thomas Nelson & Sons, Ltd.

ISBN: 0-8019-5414-2

Library of Congress Catalog Card No. 74-184139

Designed by William E. Lickfield

Manufactured in the United States of America

To Clifton
    from F.E.I.
To Jennifer
    from M.E.A.
To Chris and Claire/Danny and Chrissy
    from F.C.

Preface

The rules that determine what evidence may be presented in a court trial and the manner in which it may be used are generally referred to as "the law of evidence". In the present publication we present, in as non-legalistic a manner as possible, a discussion of the various evidentiary rules that the police are most likely to encounter in the course of their case investigations and in the testimony they may be called upon to present in court.

We trust, and believe, that this book will enhance the proficiency of investigation by the police, and at the same time increase the effectiveness of their courtroom testimony.

FRED E. INBAU
MARVIN E. ASPEN
FRANK CARRINGTON

Contents

EVIDENCE LAW
FOR
THE POLICE

Section 1

Classification of Evidence

Classification of evidence is based on simple, non-technical concepts which we hope to present in a commonsense manner. Many examples relevant to criminal law enforcement will be used in this presentation, and throughout this book. If a concept of the law of evidence appears difficult to understand at first, the reader is advised to continue reading the practical examples illustrating the various concepts, and then re-consider the concepts themselves in light of the illustrations presented.

"Evidence" is defined very simply as "the means by which facts are proved". The classification of evidence is equally simple: facts may be proved by *real evidence* or by *testimonial evidence.*

Real evidence is evidence that speaks for itself. It is a direct physical illustration of a fact. Real evidence might consist of a bullet taken from a dead body, or a gun, a bloody shirt, an automobile or even a house. Specimens of handwriting or a fingerprint lifted from a surface at a crime scene would also be considered *real evidence.*

Real evidence may consist of the actual piece of evidence itself, such as a bullet or a fingerprint, or it may be a representation of the physical evidence in the form of side-by-side photographs showing the identity of fingerprints, or a photograph of the body of the victim of a criminal homicide. This latter category of *real evidence* is called "real, demonstrative evidence" or simply "demonstrative evidence". An excellent example of such evidence is found in a 1967 Chicago case which involved the mass murder of eight student nurses. The murders occurred in their townhouse apartment, and

1

the bodies were found in various rooms. At the trial the accused murderer's movements from room to room were critical features in the prosecution's case. Obviously, the townhouse itself could not be brought into the courtroom, so a scale model of the house was used to illustrate to the judge and jury the physical set-up of the murder scene. The *real evidence*, of course, was the townhouse, but the model, properly authenticated, was *real, demonstrative* evidence.

All real evidence must be properly *authenticated* in a criminal case; it must be shown to be what the party offering it says it is. Thus, the prosecuting attorney who offers a bullet in evidence in a murder case must offer as a witness the pathologist who removed the bullet, or someone who saw it removed, and who could identify it as the bullet that hit the victim. This is *authentication*. It is provided by means of testimony that the evidence accurately represents what it is supposed to portray. Thus, the model of the townhouse in the foregoing case had to be authenticated by proof that it accurately represented the townhouse in which the murders occurred.

Photographs, maps, charts and other demonstrative evidence are likewise authenticated by proof that they show the actual scene with reasonable accuracy. The authentication of evidence, and "chain of custody," will be subsequently discussed in greater detail.

Testimonial evidence is evidence which the trier of fact, judge or jury, learns about from someone else through the spoken or written word.

Most testimonial evidence comes from the witness stand, but when someone's words or thoughts have been reduced to writing, or perhaps by means of a tape recording, the words or thoughts also may constitute testimonial evidence. An example of testimonial evidence is the story told by an eyewitness to a shooting, or a written confession by a defendant.

Testimonial evidence may be presented in the form of an entry made by an offender in his private diary.

Whereas real evidence tends to speak for itself to the trier of fact (the judge or jury), testimonial evidence must be presented through the spoken or written words of someone who can say that the writing or reproduction is true and accurate—that it actually represents what it purports to be; and the witness in most cases must speak from first-hand information. For instance, if the offered evidence is a tape recording of an alleged confession, someone must be presented as a witness who can testify that he heard the statement orally made, and that the tape recording is the same as that which he heard.

The two types of evidence, real and testimonial, may be used to prove facts *directly,* or they may be used to prove facts *indirectly* (or, stated another way, *circumstantially*).

An item of evidence proves a fact *directly* if it leads the trier of fact right to the point without the need to consider inferences or deductions.

Examples

1. Real evidence proving a fact directly:

O'Brian is on trial for aggravated assault upon Officer Allen by hitting him on the head with a sawed-off pool cue during a riot. The D.A. presents a photograph, taken and identified by a newsman, showing O'Brian hitting Officer Allen.

2. Testimonial evidence proving a fact directly:

In the same aggravated assault case against O'Brian, the D.A. offers as an eyewitness, Wayne, who testifies he saw O'Brian hit Officer Allen. Likewise, O'Brian's confession that he hit Officer Allen would be direct testimonial evidence.

In the foregoing situations the trier of fact is not required to infer or deduce anything; the evidence is *direct* between the photograph or the testimony or the confession and the hitting of Officer Allen.

On the other hand, if inferences or deductions are required, then the alleged fact is said to be established *circumstantially* (or *indirectly*).

Examples

1. Real evidence proving a fact circumstantially:

(a) In O'Brian's aggravated assault case, the D.A. offers in evidence a pool cue found on the ground near where Officer Allen was hit. The pool cue bears O'Brian's fingerprints. Both the pool cue and the fingerprints are items of *real* evidence that prove *circumstantially* that O'Brian hit Allen.

(b) The D.A. introduces into evidence a photograph, taken by a newsman, which shows Officer Allen on the ground, his head bleeding and O'Brian hurrying off with a pool cue in his hand. The photograph would be *real* evidence proving *circumstantially* that O'Brian hit Allen, because the trier of fact must make an inference from what he sees in the photograph that O'Brian hit Allen.

2. Testimonial evidence proving a fact circumstantially:

(a) The D.A. introduces witness Wilder who testifies that he heard O'Brian say, "I am going to get myself a pig", and that O'Brian then went into the crowd with his pool cue. This is *testimonial evidence* that proves *circumstantially* that O'Brian hit Allen because the trier of fact must infer or deduce from O'Brian's reported statement that he actually did hit Allen.

(b) The D.A. offers a statement signed by O'Brian in which O'Brian admits only that he was in the crowd when Officer Allen was hit. Here again, the trier of fact must infer or deduce from this statement (considered along with all the other evidence) that O'Brian did in fact hit Allen.

In the hypothetical case we have been using, the difference between the two types of proof—*direct evidence* and *circumstantial evidence*—may be diagrammed as follows:

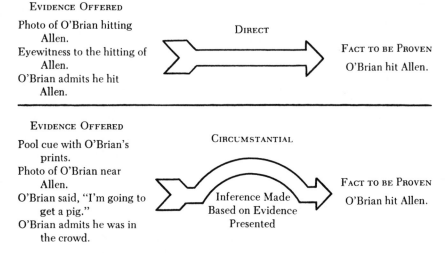

EVIDENCE OFFERED

Photo of O'Brian hitting Allen.
Eyewitness to the hitting of Allen.
O'Brian admits he hit Allen.

DIRECT

FACT TO BE PROVEN
O'Brian hit Allen.

EVIDENCE OFFERED

Pool cue with O'Brian's prints.
Photo of O'Brian near Allen.
O'Brian said, "I'm going to get a pig."
O'Brian admits he was in the crowd.

CIRCUMSTANTIAL

Inference Made Based on Evidence Presented

FACT TO BE PROVEN
O'Brian hit Allen.

It should be noted here that most criminal cases are proved circumstantially and that there is nothing wrong with this type of proof. Evidence proving a criminal case *directly* is almost exclusively confined to photographs of the actual crime (real evidence), eyewitness testimony to the actual crime (testimonial evidence) and a confession to the actual crime (testimonial evidence), but, as every police officer knows, cases of this type are in the minority. Most of the real and testimonial evidence produced by the prosecution is of an *indirect* or *circumstantial* nature; therefore, a police officer should not feel that a case which is sought to be proved indirectly or circumstantially is necessarily a weak case. There is little doubt, for example, that in our hypothetical case of the assault of Officer Allen, the fingerprints on the pool cue, or the photograph of O'Brian running away, may prove to be just as valuable as the testimony of the eyewitness, especially when consideration is given to the fallibility of the eyewitness testimony generally.

Regardless of how evidence is classified, an investigating officer should concern himself with getting *all* the available evidence and getting it in a manner that will permit its use in court. When he does this, the prosecuting attorney's prospects for convicting the criminal offender will be greatly enhanced.

Section 2

Admissibility and Weight of Evidence

During a criminal trial there are usually two determinations which must be made in regard to the consideration of evidence offered by either side. First, is the evidence *admissible?* Second, if it is admissible, what *weight* should be accorded it?

ADMISSIBILITY

The question of whether certain evidence is "admissible" is simply this: should the real or testimonial evidence (a gun or the identification testimony of a witness) be the subject of consideration by the trier of the fact, which may be either the jury or, where there is no jury, the judge himself? The judge makes this determination of admissibility even when he is also the trier of the fact, as in a non-jury case.

Ordinarily, in a jury trial, the issue arises in the following manner: as the real evidence is presented, or as a witness is asked a question by the prosecution or by defense counsel, the opposing attorney will say to the judge, "I object". Ordinarily he must do so immediately, for a delay may be looked upon as a "waiver" and the evidence is in the case even though a timely objection may have caused the judge to reject it.

In rare instances a judge may hold evidence inadmissible even though no objection is voiced by counsel. He will do this in a criminal case whenever he believes that its use would violate some substantial right of the accused.

In addition to the general requirement of a timely objection, the objecting attorney is expected to give the reasons for his objection so as to pinpoint the issue to the judge. Here, again, a waiver may be imposed upon the objecting lawyer who fails to give the reason for his objection, because if there is any legal justification whatsoever for letting the evidence in, a reviewing court usually will not fault a judge who could have kept it out for the very reason the objecting lawyer had in mind but which he failed to articulate.

If the judge decides that the tendered evidence is *admissible,* he will *overrule* the objection; if he determines that it is *inadmissible,* he will *sustain* the objection.

Under some circumstances involving the sustaining of an objection, the lawyer whose evidence is thus being kept out is required to make "an offer of proof", which means he must tell the judge what he was attempting to get into evidence and perhaps the reason why. In the absence of an "offer of proof" an erroneous ruling by the trial judge may be looked upon as inconsequential by a reviewing court; in other words, it is not likely to be considered "reversible error", because the reviewing court will not know how harmful the error may have been.

There are three cardinal rules governing the admissibility of evidence.

The first rule is that the evidence must be *competent,* that is, it must come from a reliable source. Where an extended amount of proof must be offered to establish competence, the process is called *laying a foundation.*

Example

Donald is on trial for molesting a six-year-old girl. She is the only witness against him. The judge must determine if her testimony would be competent—in other words, reliable. In this case the judge would question the little girl privately in order to see if she could remember properly, could relate adequately what she had remembered, and if she knew that it was wrong not to tell the truth. If the judge is satisfied that she meets these tests he would rule that she is competent to testify. (This same procedure would also be used if mental defectives or insane persons were to be used as witnesses.)

The second rule of evidence is that it must be *relevant,* that is, the evidence must be pertinent or applicable to a determination of a fact question in issue at the trial. In other words, does the evidence relate to the issues in the particular case?

Example

Dickenson is on trial for a theft committed in Detroit. The prosecution seeks to prove that prior to coming to Detroit, Dickerson had lived in Cincinnati, Cleveland and Indianapolis. This would be irrelevant to the issue of whether or not Dickenson had committed a theft in Detroit.

The third rule is that the evidence must be *material* to the issue. This rule is similar and in some instances identical in application to the rule of relevance. Materiality means that the evidence is not too remote from the issue in the case. It must have some probative value. In other words, would the admission of the evidence probably influence or affect significantly the decision upon the issue involved?

Example

Warren is on trial for murder by shooting with a shotgun. The prosecutor presents a witness to testify that Warren was an excellent skeet shooter. Such evidence would be relevant and material if there was an issue in the case as to whether Warren knew how to use a shotgun, or whether he was an accurate shooter, but it would not be either relevant or material in a case where the victim was shot at very close range.

These three cardinal rules are supplemented, of course, by many other rules of evidence which are to be subsequently discussed in detail. For example, the evidence may be ruled inadmissible because it is unduly prejudicial, or is against public policy, or is privileged, or was obtained by a violation of constitutional rights.

Evidence which normally would be inadmissible because of its prejudicial or inflammatory nature might nonetheless be admissible if it is competent, relevant, and material to the issues in the case. For instance, a color photograph of a murder victim might ordinarily be inadmissible because of the inflammatory (prejudicial) effect it might have on the jury, but it could be ruled admissible if color in the photograph was needed to adequately show the nature of the wound in a case where its nature may be helpful in determining whether it was or was not self-inflicted.

WEIGHT

By *weight* of the evidence is meant the degree of believability or persuasiveness, from 0 to 100%, that the trier of fact may attribute to it once it has been ruled admissible. This evaluation is made by the jury in a jury case, and by the judge in a trial without a jury. The latter is usually referred to as a *bench trial*.

Example

Lionel is on trial for a murder to which he had confessed to the police. Before the confession can be offered into evidence the judge conducts a "preliminary hearing", out of the presence of the jury, to determine whether the proper legal procedures in obtaining the confession were followed. If he decides they were not, he will rule that the confession is *inadmissible*, after which no further mention may be made of it to the jury. If the judge holds that the confession is *admissible*, the jury returns to the courtroom and they hear evidence as to how it was obtained so that they can decide what significance, if any, they will attach to it; in other words, they will decide what *weight* it should receive. For instance, if they believe Lionel's testimony that he made the false confession only to protect his wife, or that it was forced out of him, the jury may disregard it, even though the judge had decided earlier that it could be "admitted" as evidence.

Section 3

Judicial Notice

Judicial notice is an evidentiary "short-cut". The doctrine permits a court to consider something to be a fact without the necessity of producing the customary formal proof by sworn witnesses, authenticated documents, and the like.

If a fact is a matter of *common knowledge,* it would be a waste of time and money to require formal proof of that fact during the course of a trial. The court, therefore, will take judicial notice of it. The common knowledge within the community is sufficient.

> *Example*
>
> Martin is on trial in a Chicago court for involuntary manslaughter occasioned when he ran a red light on State Street in Chicago and hit a pedestrian. The judge could take judicial notice that State Street is one of the main thoroughfares in downtown Chicago.

Even though a fact may not be a matter of common knowledge, if it is *capable of accurate and ready demonstration,* it may be accorded judicial notice.

> *Example*
>
> In State X, officers are prohibited from executing search warrants at night unless the affidavit or complaint for the search warrant states *positively* that the property to be searched for is on the premises to be searched. In a motion to suppress evidence in State X, it is material as to whether officers entered to execute a warrant in the daytime or nighttime. The judge could refer to the world almanac to find out

10

the official time of sunrise and sunset on the date in question
and he could take judicial notice of the time therein.

A state court will usually take judicial notice of its own state laws
and federal laws, and in some jurisdictions, but not all, those of another state. A state court will not take judicial notice of a municipal
ordinance; however, a municipal court will take judicial notice of
its own city ordinances.

Section 4

Presumptions and Burden of Proof

In a criminal case the defendant is presumed to be innocent and the prosecution has the burden of proving his guilt *beyond a reasonable doubt.*

Many courts refuse to define "reasonable doubt", saying, in effect, that the term is self-explanatory. One court put it this way: "There is no more lucid definition of the term 'reasonable doubt' than the term itself."

Although reasonable doubt cannot be defined in mathematical terms or percentages (i.e., 99% sure is beyond reasonable doubt), it is safe to say that the term simply means that degree of doubt which would prevent a reasonable and just man from coming to a conclusion of guilt.

In a civil case the burden of proof rests upon the plaintiff, the party who filed the suit, but he need only prove his case by a "preponderance of the evidence." This means that in order for the plaintiff to win his case he must convince the jury (or the judge) that there is more "weight" to his evidence than that presented by the plaintiff.

The Burden of Proof Rule in Ordinance Violation Cases

Municipalities, counties and other state political subdivisions have legislation similar to state statutes, called "ordinances". Technically, they are referred to as "quasi-criminal" in nature; in other words, *almost,* but not quite, criminal. They provide punishment for wrongful but non-criminal conduct.

12

A vehicular parking regulation is an example of the conduct governed by ordinances. The penalty for violating an ordinance is usually only a fine.

In an ordinance violation trial, the prosecution must prove its case by a *"clear* preponderance of the evidence." This is a somewhat greater requirement than the *simple* preponderance of the evidence in a civil case, but it is a lesser requirement than proof beyond a reasonable doubt as in a criminal case.

THE BURDEN OF "GOING FORWARD WITH THE EVIDENCE"

The burden of "going forward with the evidence" is different from burden of proof as such. The burden of going forward with the evidence is the obligation to introduce evidence to meet that of the opposing party, or more likely, to overcome presumptions arising from facts. This burden of going forward will normally relate to a particular piece of evidence, whereas burden of proof generally relates to the ultimate issue in the case. The burden of going forward with evidence may shift from the prosecution to the defendant; the burden of proof, however, is always upon the prosecution.

In certain types of situations, where evidence is more readily obtainable by the defendant than by the prosecution, the burden of producing that evidence may shift to him, as long as this obligation will not subject him to hardship or oppression. Examples of this are the so-called "affirmative defenses", such as insanity, alibi, infancy, intoxication. In matters of this nature, the defendant usually has the burden of going forward with evidence in support of that particular defense. However, once his evidence is submitted, the prosecution must prove the contrary to be true.

PRESUMPTIONS

In addition to the important, constitutional presumption of innocence, there are various other kinds of presumptions, most of which operate against the defendant.

Presumptions ordinarily will not make out a case against an accused person; they only help. Whenever a presumption exists (either created by statute or court decision), some move thereafter is expected from the defendant. It may come in the form of his own rebutting testimony, or from some other witness or evidence.

Example

Lewis is on trial for murder. A presumption exists that every person is sane. Consequently, if insanity is to be an issue, Lewis must present *some* evidence, even though it may be rather flimsy, that he is insane, after which the prosecution has the burden of proving that he is sane.

A basic rule with regard to presumptions is that there must be a "rational connection" between a proved fact and the inference that is drawn from it. In other words, when one thing is proved, before anything can be presumed or inferred from it, there must be a sound reason for doing so. A few illustrations will make this point clear.

Example

A statute provides that the presence of a machine gun in any room or dwelling house shall be presumptive evidence of its illegal possession by all of the persons occupying the place. Smith, Jones, and Brown share an apartment together. A lawful court warrant search discloses a machine gun. All three are guilty of its possession; it is highly unlikely that a machine gun could be in the apartment without each one of them knowing of its presence.

Example

A statute prohibits the carrying of a pistol in any automobile. Green, White, Black, and Brown are in Green's automobile which he is driving. A lawfully conducted search of the car uncovers a pistol under a towel on the front seat between Green and White. All four occupants are charged for violation of the statute. Although Green and White may be guilty, Black and Brown are not, because it is unreasonable to presume that they knew of the presence of the gun. Proof would have to be forthcoming that they were actually aware of its presence. As for Green and White, however, the presumption is valid.

Example

A federal statute provides that it is unlawful to possess marijuana or heroin illegally imported into the United States, and it further provides that the possessor is deemed to know of its unlawful importation. (The reason for basing the offense upon the act of importation is to establish federal jurisdiction. A state, of course, can make possession a crime regardless of whether the possessor knew of the substance's illegal importation.)

Henry is found with marijuana in his coat pocket. Davis is found with heroin.

The presumption of illegal importation is invalid as to Henry and his marijuana, but valid for Davis and his heroin. The reason for this distinction is that marijuana grows in this country, whereas the source of heroin is almost invariably abroad.

TRAFFIC OFFENSE PRESUMPTIONS

In most states there are two presumptions common to traffic offenses:

(1) The person who illegally parked the automobile is presumed to be the owner. This presumption is the basis of the "hang-on" traffic ticket (notice to appear). However, this presumption, like any other, can be rebutted. For example, in many states, a traffic citation for illegal parking issued to a car rental company will be discharged where the company can show that its agents and employees did not have control of the vehicle on the date the violation occurred.

(2) The individual found intoxicated behind the wheel of a parked vehicle (with the motor running or ignition key turned on), or behind the wheel of a wrecked vehicle, is presumed to have driven it while under the influence of alcohol. In some states the above described circumstantial evidence creates a presumption which, if left unrebutted, is sufficient to establish the corpus delicti of the offense. Again, as with any presumption, it is rebuttable. For example, the accused could offer evidence that he parked the car *prior* to drinking the alcohol.

Section 5

The Hearsay Rule

Suppose a neighbor tells your wife something that another neighbor told her regarding an incident in a supermarket one Saturday morning. It involved a fracas between one husband/wife couple and another husband/wife couple. If you were interested in getting a factual account of what occurred, would you settle for the information your wife transmits to you? Or would you prefer to get the story from someone who was in the store and saw and heard what happened?

We think you would prefer to hear from the first-hand witness rather than from anyone else. If the story comes to you second-hand you almost instinctively realize the risk of unreliability. You would also realize that you would have no way of testing the second or third-hand witness as to the accuracy of the related version of the incident. You would be unable to ask questions by way of, shall we say, "cross-examination", because the person talking to you, your wife in this case, did not witness the incident herself and could only be "cross-examined" as to whether she heard correctly and related accurately what she heard. But she cannot be cross-examined as to her own knowledge about such things as who started the fracas, who was injured, and the extent of the injuries. This, we suggest, is the reason for the "hearsay rule" in the law of evidence —the general rule which, in most cases, excludes all but first-hand information.

The hearsay rule requires that when a witness in court tells of facts, circumstances, and events, he should speak only about those facts, circumstances and events of which he has *personal knowl-*

edge. Stated in its simplest terms: the court and jury want to hear what *he knows;* not what someone *told him.*

Phrased in legalistic terms, the hearsay rule may be described as one which prohibits the use in evidence of an assertion of an alleged fact unless the person to whom the assertion is attributed is available for cross-examination by the party adversely affected by it.

The reason for the traditional insistence upon the right of cross-examination is to guard against untruthful or unreliable evidence. In other words, a person who takes the witness stand and testifies to certain alleged facts based upon his own personal observations or experiences may be cross-examined about such matters as his physical or psychological capacity to have made an accurate observation of the occurrence or event in question. For instance, was he really able to see one person hit another from the place where he said he was standing at the time? Was his eyesight good enough? Was he or was he not wearing his contact lenses at the time? Was he so shaken up psychologically by preceding events that he was unable to maintain his composure to observe accurately the main occurrence he purports to have observed? Is his relation to the defendant, or to the crime victim, such that he may have a motive to lie as he relates his testimony? Or might he, by virtue of some other factor, be subject to an unconscious incentive to distort the truth? Or could he have been bribed to say what he said on direct examination?

Inquiries into any one or more such possibilities may result in a disregard by the court or jury of part or all of what the witness said on direct examination when he was being questioned by a friendly attorney. However, few if any of the foregoing opportunities are available to the adverse party if all the witness testifies to is what someone told him. He can be cross-examined, of course, as to whether he is telling the truth about what someone told him, but beyond that there is nothing more to be disclosed; he cannot be asked anything about the occurrence or the event itself, for the simple reason that he was not there to obtain first-hand information. Consequently, the courts as a general rule insist upon first-hand information.

Example

Jackson tells the police that Dennis told him that Burns killed Thomas. At Burns's trial Jackson will not be permitted to testify as to what Dennis told him; he himself does not *know* from his own independent knowledge that Burns killed Thomas, nor can he be cross-examined about the killing since the limit of his information is what Dennis *told* him.

Example

Brown is on trial for shooting Smith. Wilcox takes the witness stand and says: "I saw Brown shoot Smith". Brown's attorney on cross-examination can question Wilcox fully in order to see if he is telling the truth, if he observed the situation correctly, if he has any reason to lie. Wilcox's testimony would not be hearsay because Wilcox is now speaking of his own knowledge.

Example

Officer Williams arrests Hales for the theft of an automobile he is driving. Hales admits that the car was stolen by his friend Ganz and that he was with Ganz at the time of the theft.

Ganz is arrested and both he and Hales are charged with theft. No attempt was made to interrogate Ganz, or to obtain any evidence of his guilt beyond what Hales had said and acknowledged in a written, signed confession.

Upon arraignment, Hales and Ganz both plead not guilty. For reasons subsequently explained, separate trials are ordered. Without Hales's testimony as a witness in court, the prosecution of Ganz would fail. The hearsay rule would prohibit the use of Hales's confession against Ganz.

The last example is illustrative of a mistake frequently made by investigating officers—the acceptance by them of an out-of-court statement as the equivalent of proof of the facts related. In such instances as the one related in this example, the proper investigative procedure to follow would be to interrogate the implicated person, Ganz, and if he denies his guilt then attempt to secure some other proof of the theft. In any event, it would be a futile gesture to prosecute Ganz by relying solely upon Hales's statement of implication.

This mistake may also occur in cases where the investigator may tell a suspect that he will be given a pass if he identifies the major participant in the crime and reveals all he knows about it. Any such statement by an accomplice, standing alone, would be valueless evidence, however much it would help as a police investigative aid.

Hearsay and Non-Hearsay Distinguished

One very important point about the hearsay rule must be remembered. It is only applicable to those cases in which we are concerned with whether or not what the declarant said was *truthful* or *accurate*. In some cases it is of no consequence whether the statement of the declarant was truthful or not; the only fact of interest is whether or not he said it. In these cases the hearsay rule does not apply.

Example

Arnold, a chemist, tells his friend Phillips that he has felt a big lump in his throat and that he is sure it is cancerous because his father died of throat cancer. That night Arnold is found dead of potassium cyanide poisoning. His wife, also a chemist, is suspected and accused of killing him, because the investigation reveals she was having an affair with another man, and she had been heard to say she would like to get rid of Arnold.

At the trial of Arnold's wife, Phillips may testify about what Arnold had said. Whether Arnold did or did not have a cancerous lump in his neck is immaterial; however, his concern over cancer may have caused him to commit suicide, a factor obviously deserving of consideration in a case where someone is being tried for his murder.

The foregoing example also illustrates another feature of the hearsay rule—the statement credited to the wife that she would like to get rid of Arnold. Although legal scholars differ as to whether statements attributed to a defendant in a criminal case are outside the hearsay rule, or admissible as an exception to it, the fact remains that any out-of-court statement made by a defendant that is relevant to the issue in the case can be offered in evidence against him.

Where a party to a lawsuit, either criminal or civil, has had a prior opportunity to cross-examine a witness, that witness's previously given testimony may be used in a subsequent trial even though he is not then available for another cross-examination.

Example

As a "rookie" policeman, Officer Davis was assigned to the narcotics squad as an undercover agent. He made several "buys" of narcotics from Sampson, a pusher. At Sampson's trial Davis testified under oath about the "buys" and was cross-examined by counsel for Sampson. Sampson was convicted, but his conviction was reversed because of an erroneous instruction given to the jury by the judge. Meanwhile Davis has been drafted into military service and at the time of Sampson's second trial is in a foreign country. Davis's original testimony may be introduced in evidence at the second trial because of the prior opportunity for cross-examination.

Exceptions to the Hearsay Rule

Exceptions to the hearsay rule have been developed over the years because of one primary consideration—the strong probability that the statement which is sought to be used as evidence is a truthful one and there is no compelling need to cross-examine the person who is alleged to have made it. The best example, insofar as the police are concerned, is the so-called dying declaration.

Dying Declarations

As previously stated, the hearsay rule prohibits the use in evidence of an out-of-court statement to prove the truthfulness of an alleged fact unless the person who made the statement is available for cross-examination by the party adversely affected by it. How, then, may the prosecution in a homicide case, put in evidence the dying declaration of the victim who obviously is no longer available for cross-examination? Moreover, what about the constitutional right of an accused person to be confronted with the witness against him?

The right of cross-examination may be dispensed with *if* there is some *adequate substitute for the truth disclosing quality of cross-examination itself.* And it is upon this basis that a dying declaration may be admitted into evidence, under certain conditions to be mentioned shortly.

The legal theory supporting the admissibility of dying declarations is that a person who is about to die will be reluctant to die with a lie on his lips, largely as a result of a possible belief in the hereafter; consequently, there is a high probability that what he says at that time is the truth. Despite this premise, however, several requirements have been laid down before a dying declaration will be accepted as evidence, some of them undoubtedly the result of a lack of full confidence in the basic premise that all people are afraid to die with a lie on their lips. They are as follows:

1. The person making the statement—referred to in the courtroom as *the declarant*—must have lost all hope of recovery. A mere belief in the probability that he will die is insufficient; death to him must be a *certainty*.

By what means can this belief in certain death be legally established? Must the declarant actually acknowledge that belief orally or in writing if he is unable to speak? In the absence of his own acknowledgment, must some doctor tell him that he is going to die? Or, are there other available means?

Although an actual expression of an awareness of impending death is perhaps the most reliable evidence of that belief, it, nevertheless, may be established circumstantially—as when a physician tells the injured person that there is no hope of survival, or when the fatal nature of the injury is very apparent to everyone.

2. Another requirement for the admissibility of a dying declaration is the rather obvious one that at the time it is sought to be used as evidence, the declarant must in fact be dead. If he surprised himself and others by surviving, the statement is unusable as evidence, regardless of a sound and genuine belief that death was inevitable at the time it was made. Since he is now available for cross-examination, no substitute for that opportunity is needed or acceptable.

Although the two foregoing rules make good sense, there are certain questionable limitations which a number of courts have imposed upon the use of dying declarations:

3. A dying declaration can only be used in a criminal prosecution for the killing of the declarant himself.

4. Only that part of the declaration can be used which relates to the circumstances that led immediately to the death.

To the second question raised at the outset of this discussion of dying declarations (the matter of the constitutional right of confrontation), all that need be mentioned is this: the right of confrontation simply means that there must be an opportunity to cross-examine an adverse witness *if he is alive* and thus available for cross-examination, so as to permit the adverse party to test the trustworthiness of what he says. If however, there is a satisfactory substitute for this assurance of trustworthiness, the confrontation element is satisfied. Upon this reasoning, dying declarations have long been held not to violate the constitutional right of confrontation.

Example

Officer Mills, called to the scene of a stabbing, finds Walters seriously wounded and rushes him to a hospital. On the way there, Walters tells Mills: "It's no use; I'm a goner. Jameson stabbed me; he also tried to drown me two weeks ago. Ask my father to take care of my wife and kids." Two hours later, Walters dies in the hospital.

At Jameson's trial, Officer Mills may testify that Walters said Jameson stabbed him. However, he will not be permitted to testify about the drowning attempt, since it is unrelated to the circumstance that led to Walters' death.

Example

Officer Jensen, called to the scene of a shooting, finds Austin with a bullet wound in his abdomen. Jensen rushes him to the hospital, and Austin, fully conscious, is taken to the emergency room. About an hour later Doctor Wood comes out of the emergency room and tells Officer Jensen, "It's no use—he's dying". Officer Jensen then enters the emergency room and asks Austin who shot him. Austin replies, "Donaldson shot me", and dies.

Austin's declaration would not be admissible because there is no evidence that he knew that he was dying. The doctor told Officer Jensen, not Austin, that Austin was dying, and for a dying declaration to be admissible it is the declarant himself who must know that he is dying.

Example

While on a hunting trip, Welford is the victim of a shotgun blast that tore off half of his abdomen. The shooting occurred in a cabin to which he and his two companions, Smith and Jones, had to walk rather than reach by car. When Smith comes to the cabin after hearing the shot, he finds Welford writhing in a large pool of blood with his intestines hanging out. He asks Welford what happened and Welford replies, "Jones shot me". An hour later Welford dies.

The statement can be used at Jones's trial for killing Welford. Even though Welford never acknowledged he was going to die, the circumstances and the severity of the wound clearly indicated that certainty and he must have realized he could not survive.

Spontaneous ("Res Gestae") Declarations

We parenthesize the term "res gestae" because of the popularity of the expression rather than because of anything else. Literally, the phrase means "things done". However, "res gestae" has come to stand for a group of basic reasons for holding certain declarations admissible in evidence as exceptions to the hearsay rule. Those reasons are all founded upon the premise that declarations may be uttered under some circumstances that insure their trustworthiness, and, consequently, the courts are willing to dispense with the protection usually afforded by the opportunity for cross-examination.

About the only type of hearsay exception declarations that are of practical concern to the police officer are those that may be referred to as "spontaneous" or "excited utterances"—utterances made at the time of or immediately after an exciting or startling event.

Example

Paulson is stabbed in the back. As the assailant is fleeing, a person who witnessed the act yells "That fellow did it!". The witness then gets in his car and leaves. Bates, who heard the exclamation of the witness, takes off after "that fellow" and apprehends him. The witness disappears completely and is not heard from again.

At the trial of the accused stabber, Bates may testify about the unknown witness's exclamation. It was an excited utterance and is considered trustworthy enough to be used as evidence of the assailant's identity even though the declarant himself is unavailable for cross-examination.

Example

In the foregoing factual situation, assume that the unknown witness made no exclamation at the time but an hour later he tells somebody that "the fellow who was arrested is the man who stabbed Paul". Because of the lapse of time and the lack of "spontaneity", that declaration could not be used in evidence as a substitute for the witness's actual testimony.

Example

A woman is raped and stabbed. As her attacker is fleeing she yells out "Johnson did this to me!" At the time of the declaration the victim had no idea the wound was fatal. Even though the statement obviously would not be a dying declaration, because she did not know she was dying, it could be used as an excited utterance. The spontaneity itself is a guarantee of its trustworthiness. (We should point out, however, that the declaration alone would not be proof of Johnson's guilt beyond a reasonable doubt; all we intend to convey is that it could be used along with other evidence submitted in the case.)

In certain types of occurrences the quality of spontaneity is not lost by the mere fact that the declaration came in response to a question someone asked such as "What happened?" The test is whether at that time the state of excitement was still high.

REGULAR ENTRIES IN THE COURSE OF BUSINESS

Another exception to the hearsay rule is the regular entry in the course of business. To qualify, the entry must have been made at the time of the business as part of a series of transactions. It must be shown that the entry was made with the personal knowledge of the person making it, or, if not so made, it must have been made in the course of a regular bookkeeping system. Under the "Uniform Business Records as Evidence Act", in force in most states, the court must also be convinced of the fairness and reliability of the record.

The courts make this exception to the hearsay rule on the theory that since no controversy existed at the time the entry was made, there was no motivation to falsify the record. Of course, if such controversy did exist, the exception would not prevail.

The original entry must be offered into evidence. A transcript or summary of the record will not usually be permitted as a substitute for the original.

Example

McManus, the dock foreman at a large discount sales company, is on trial for conspiring with a gang of thieves to steal items enroute to customers from the company's loading dock. Inventory sheets prepared by the shipping department, properly authenticated by the employee who made the entries on the sheets, would be admissible as regular entries in the course of business to prove the amount and value of the items taken.

Example

Same facts as above except that Sampson, the employee in the shipping department responsible for keeping the inventory ledgers, is also on trial with McManus for conspiring with him to cover up the thefts by falsifying inventory records. Now, since there is a controversy over the reliability of the shipping records, due to Sampson's obvious motivation to falsify them, this exception to the hearsay rule would not apply and the amounts and values in question would have to be proved from other sources.

PUBLIC RECORDS

Records kept by public officials usually are admissible in evidence as an exception to the hearsay rule. The exception was created upon the premise that the persons making the records have no motive to falsify and that the records are open to public inspection. The courts also have taken into consideration that, in many instances, the persons who make the entries are unavailable.

The criteria set forth by the courts for the admission into evidence of a public record as an exception to the hearsay rule are: (1) the public official is required by law to keep the record; and (2) he made them in the course of his official duties, or under his general supervision by some person in his employ.

In most instances a certified copy of the record may be admitted rather than the original recording itself.

The courts will usually delete opinion or other improper evidence from the public record before admitting it. For example, the coroner's notation on a death certificate that the fatal gunshot wound was in his opinion self-inflicted would be deleted prior to the admission into evidence of this public record.

Example

State Y's "habitual criminal" statute provides that upon the fourth conviction of any felony the defendant may be sentenced to life imprisonment. Evans has just been found guilty of robbery. At his sentencing the prosecutor, invoking the "habitual criminal" act, may introduce certified copies of the records of Evans's three prior felony convictions.

MATTERS OF PEDIGREE

Evidence relating to matters of birth, death, marriage and family relationship are admissible in a not too frequently evoked exception to the hearsay rule. Where there are no records of the event in question, the court will admit hearsay testimony as to these matters of pedigree on the theory that the statements are trustworthy because they occurred before the controversy arose. The courts also state that, because this hearsay testimony is the only way matters of pedigree can be shown, the exception will be allowed.

These hearsay statements as to birth, death, marriage or family relationship are usually restricted by the courts to members of the family, old friends and family servants. The hearsay statement will be admitted only when the person who originally uttered it is dead or wholly unavailable. And as noted above, the statement must have been made at a time prior to the establishment of the controversy in question.

Example

Corneal is being tried for having sexual relations in 1968 with Cheryl, a girl under the age of 18. There is some doubt as to her age and her parents are dead. Mrs. Zinn, a close friend of Cheryl's family, could testify that Cheryl's mother told her, Mrs. Zinn, that Cheryl was born on the day that "Mr. Eisenhower took over the Presidency from Mr. Truman" (January 20, 1952, Inauguration Day) in order to show that Cheryl was not in fact 18 when Corneal had sexual relations with her.

Section 6

The Best-Evidence Rule

A rule of evidence was created many years ago with respect to *written documents,* which required that proof of the contents of a writing could only be made by producing the *original* document itself, unless it was unavailable for some reason other than a serious fault of the person who sought to prove its contents. The soundness of this rule becomes obvious when we consider the natural inability of human beings to observe accurately, remember accurately, and relate accurately what they have read. A slight variance between the written statement and an oral report of its contents could have particularly serious consequences with regard to legal documents such as a contract, deed, or will, or, in criminal cases, a threatening letter, other alleged written evidence of a criminal offense, or even a confession. Significant risks may be involved even with submitted copies of a handwritten or typewritten document. Consequently, the courts insist that whenever possible the original document itself be produced. In instances where the written document is unavailable—as when it has been destroyed by an accidental fire— then and only then, may a carbon or photocopy be used as evidence.

Example

A raid on a syndicate gambling operation netted a large quantity of gambling bet records; however, at the trial of the case, during a recess, all of the seized records were stolen from the courtroom. Fortunately, an alert vice detective had made copies of all of the bet records. Obviously, the original records were the "best evidence" of the bets contained

27

thereon, but since they were no longer available the copies which the detective had made were admissible to prove the bets.

The best-evidence rule is not applicable to things other than documents, unless they themselves contain writings which are relevant to the present case. In the latter situation there may be a need to produce the original object itself, but, even then, to produce or not to produce the object itself will rest within the discretion of the trial judge.

Example

During the course of a bank robbery fingerprints are left on a counter. Fingerprint technicians powder the prints and photograph them. The photographs are admissible and there is no need to produce the wood or slab upon which they were found.

Example

An automobile engine is stolen. The thieves sand off the serial number and stamp on a forged number. When the engine is recovered, police technicians apply an etching chemical to restore the original serial number. They then photograph that area of the engine block to show the original number as well as the forged one.

Strictly speaking, this case involves a "writing," for which the best-evidence rule may be applicable. However, the trial judge may—and undoubtedly would—exercise his discretion and not require that the engine itself be produced.

With regard to the application of the best-evidence rule to confessions, it may be said that if it is a written and signed document or a tape recorded one, and the prosecution wants to make its contents known to the court and jury, the original would have to be produced. Neither a copy nor an oral report of its contents would be acceptable. On the other hand, however, testimony would be received of a prior oral confession, just so long as reliance is placed upon its contents rather than the contents of the written or otherwise recorded one.

Example

Howard is arrested for robbery. After receiving the necessary *Miranda* warnings he is interrogated and he confesses to the robbery. His confession is reduced to writing and signed by him.

The officer who obtained the written confession will not be permitted to relate its contents orally; the written confession "speaks for itself" and is the best evidence of its contents.

The officer may nevertheless relate what Howard said earlier, and that will be admissible regardless of whether or not the written confession itself is offered as evidence.

Section 7

Present Memory Refreshed and Past Recollection Recorded

In general, when an officer testifies at a trial, the facts and circumstances of the case will be reasonably fresh in his mind and he will not need to consult, on the witness stand, any notes or reports he might have previously made about the incident. However, situations may arise in which an officer will need to refer to his notes, because (a) there has been a lengthy time lapse between the event and the trial; (b) the case involved a wealth of detail; or (c) the officer handles so many of the type of case in which he is testifying that he cannot remember one from another for very long. In such cases, two procedures for the use of notes, reports or memoranda by the officer-witness are permissible.

PRESENT MEMORY REFRESHED

The first instance in which an officer will refer to his notes during the course of his testimony is a procedure called *present memory refreshed.* Under this procedure, before the officer-witness is permitted to refer to his notes while on the witness stand, he must testify that he does not recall or has only a hazy recollection as to the matter about which he is being questioned; and he must also state that there is a memorandum which he or some other person had previously prepared which would aid in refreshing his recollection about this matter.

The prosecutor then will request that the officer-witness examine the document. Afterwards, the prosecutor will ask him whether the examination of that document has refreshed his recollection. If the
30

answer is "yes", the officer will continue his oral testimony about the matter in question.

Example

Nelson is a U.S. Treasury Agent, assigned to undercover operations involving illicit gambling activities. During the months of September, October, and November of 1969, he infiltrated a gambling ring in a local tavern, and placed bets with bookies there on an almost daily basis. As a result of this investigation, the tavern was raided and the bookmakers charged with gambling.

The trial takes place in June 1971. Nelson takes the stand, identifies himself, describes the overall pattern of the bookie operation, and tells that each day after leaving the tavern he wrote down an account of every bet he placed that day—the name of the horse, the park and race, the amount of the bet, with whom the bet was made. The prosecutor asks him to describe each bet in detail. After requesting the court for permission to refresh his memory, he consults the notes which he had made for the details of the bets and proceeds to testify. In so doing he testifies from his own memory about the overall operation, but he has refreshed his memory by the record he kept of the individual bets made. Both the lapse of time between the investigation and the amount of detail involved would justify his refreshing his memory.

Example

A homicide detective who made a crime scene search is called upon to testify as to what he observed and found at the scene. He may use his notes which he made at the scene in order to refresh his recollection of such details as the distance between the body and other objects, the position of the body, the location of the weapon, and the location and configuration of blood spots.

The trial judge will usually permit defense counsel to examine the document used to refresh the witness's recollection, and he may, of course, cross-examine the witness as to the accuracy of his recollection. The document itself, however, may not be offered in evidence to be examined and considered by the jury.

PAST RECOLLECTION RECORDED

The second instance where an officer-witness is permitted to refer to a memorandum on the witness stand is called *past recollection recorded.* This procedure is often invoked when his present memory cannot be refreshed—for instance, where he testifies that even after examining the document that he himself prepared, he has no present independent recollection of the events described in the document.

Under the doctrine of *past recollection recorded,* the document itself will be admissible in evidence *if* (a) after examining the document, he states that he cannot independently recall the events noted, but that (b) he made the notes himself, and that they (c) were made at the same time or very soon after the events described, and that (d) even though he has no independent recollection of the facts noted, he knows that the notes were correct at the time he made them.

Although *past recollection recorded* permits the introduction of the document into evidence, the witness in these circumstances will not be permitted to testify as to the contents of the document. The document will speak for itself and is the best evidence of its contents.

> *Example*
>
> Officer Garson of the Accident Investigations Division of a large police department investigates three or four accidents a day, and he may be subpoenaed to testify about them six to eight months later. He may remember the major accidents well enough to testify about them from a refreshing of his memory as above described, but in the hundreds of "fender bender" cases which he has investigated he literally will not remember anything about them. In such instances, he merely testifies that he made the accident report on such and such a date, that it was made contemporaneous to the event, and that the facts were correctly recorded at the time he wrote the report. This is sufficient to have the accident report read at the trial.

In summary, a police officer will usually testify from his independent recollection. If he is unable to do so, he may refer to notes to refresh his recollection. But if his recollection is not refreshed by referring to these notes, the notes themselves will be admitted into evidence where they have been made by the officer himself under the above described conditions.

It should be noted here, parenthetically, that there is nothing wrong with the use of either present memory refreshed or past recollection recorded. No one expects a police officer to be a walking IBM machine and, obviously, a busy officer will not remember every detail of every case on which he has worked. On the other hand, correct trial preparation requires that an officer review his notes, reports, and memoranda before he takes the witness stand in order to be prepared to testify properly about the subject, and to use those materials, if necessary, while testifying.

Section 8

The Exclusionary (Illegally
Seized Evidence) Rule

In 1914, the Supreme Court of the United States ruled that if federal law enforcement officers obtained incriminating evidence by illegal means, the evidence could not be used in a federal prosecution against the person from whose possession it was taken. The purpose of the rule was to discourage illegal police practices.

This *exclusionary rule* was first established by an invocation of the Supreme Court's "supervisory power" over lower federal courts (and indirectly, therefore, over federal law enforcement officers). Since that was the basis for the rule, rather than a constitutional requirement, the state courts were at liberty either to use or not to use the exclusionary rule in state criminal trials. Given this option, about half of the states adopted it; the others rejected it. But in 1961 this option was removed by the Supreme Court decision in *Mapp v. Ohio*, which held that the Constitution's Fourth Amendment prohibited "unreasonable searches and seizures" and required that *all* courts, state as well as federal, refuse to allow courtroom use to be made of anything illegally obtained from the accused by law enforcement officers. Today, therefore, all state courts must follow the exclusionary rule, including the state of Michigan whose own constitution had allowed use to be made of illegally seized evidence obtained during street searches involving firearms and narcotics.

> *Example*
> Officers Jenkins and Watson have a "hunch" that Alfred is a seller of narcotics. They stop him and reach into his coat pockets where they find narcotics and also a house key.

While Jenkins keeps Alfred in custody, Watson uses the key to enter Alfred's home. A search of his house reveals more narcotics and also a number of stolen transistor radios, all of which are seized.

None of the evidence can be used in a prosecution of Alfred. It was all illegally seized and will be suppressed. This, in practical effect, means that Alfred goes free.

The stated objective of the United States Supreme Court in suppressing such evidence is "to teach the police a lesson", so that they will only arrest and search a person upon probable cause or reasonable grounds, rather than upon a mere "hunch", and that they will obtain a search warrant before entering and searching a home under circumstances illustrated in the present example.

The legal procedure by which illegally seized evidence is kept out of a case is by defense counsel filing a pre-trial *motion to suppress* such evidence. During the *preliminary hearing* upon this issue the prosecution must satisfy the judge that the evidence was properly obtained. If he succeeds, the evidence is declared to be admissible at the trial; if he fails, the evidence is suppressed.

Although in former years the prosecution had no right to appeal from a trial court suppression order, in many states (and in the federal courts in certain cases), either by legislation or by court decision, that right is presently available.

Example

A trial judge, either through ignorance of the law, or because of sheer corruptness, grants a pre-trial *motion to suppress* gambling paraphernalia seized by an officer who was admitted into a gambling establishment along with other persons patronizing the joint.

Under the earlier rule, this action on the part of the trial judge would have the effect of freeing the operator of the gambling joint. Now, in many jurisdictions, an appeal can be taken from the ruling of the trial judge. If his ruling is reversed a trial may then be conducted and the evidence used.

The exclusionary rule is not restricted in its application to physical objects such as gambling paraphernalia, weapons, and narcotics; it applies as well to all other illegally seized evidence.

Example

Arnold, under arrest for rape, voluntarily confesses to the crime. Prior to his confession, however, the police interroga-

tor had failed to give him the *Miranda* warnings. Consequently the confession will be suppressed. Unless there is
ample other evidence of guilt beyond a reasonable doubt,
Arnold goes free.

In addition to not being permitted to use the illegally seized evidence itself, prosecutors cannot make any *derivative use* of such evidence.

Example

The police make an illegal entry into Reed's home after
suspecting him of selling narcotics. Although they find no
narcotics they do see Sarah Hensley there, whom they know
to be an addict. In her purse she has a syringe and a hypodermic needle.

Sarah agrees to testify that she had bought some heroin
from Reed and had injected a shot in her arm just before the
police had arrived. Reed's motion to suppress Sarah's testimony will be allowed because the awareness of her testimony
was derived from the illegal entry into Reed's home.

Example FBI

The police, without legal authorization, "bug" Garland's
hotel room. They hear him describe to a friend how he burglarized a home. They hear him say that he hid the loot in a
tree trunk in a forest preserve. The police find the loot there.

At a pre-trial hearing the court will not only suppress the
incriminating statements Garland made, but also the evidence of the loot.

(The loot, of course, would not be given back to Garland
since it is "contraband" and will be "confiscated" and returned to the rightful owner. The courts have not gone so far
as to say that it must be given to the burglar to *really* teach
the police a lesson.)

A few courts (the California Supreme Court, for instance) have
extended the application of the exclusionary rule to cover not only
evidence illegally obtained from the defendant himself, from his
home or place of business, but also evidence illegally seized from
somebody else.

Example

An illegal police entry is made into Finch's home. In it
they find stolen property on which fingerprints are developed
that are later identified as the fingerprints of Gates. At

Gates's trial for theft (in states such as California), he could
have the fingerprint evidence suppressed because of the illegal entry into Finch's home.

The basis for this extension of the exclusionary rule is that if its purpose is to teach the police a lesson, it should not be restricted in its application to illegal police conduct toward the defendant, but should also require the suppression of *all* illegally seized evidence, regardless of the person who was subjected to the illegal conduct.

There is substantial opposition to the exclusionary rule. Its opponents feel that there are better ways to protect citizens against illegal police conduct than by turning factually guilty persons loose in order to teach the police a lesson. If and when such a viewpoint materializes, it will probably come about by a constitutional amendment rather than by court action. It is conceivable, however, that the Supreme Court might overrule its 5-4 decision in *Mapp v. Ohio* which elevated the rule from an evidentiary one into a constitutional requirement, and thereby once again permit the state courts or their legislatures, or even the Congress of the United States, to determine whether or not it is a necessary device for the control of police misconduct.

Section 9

The Self-Incrimination Privilege

A person who is asked a question that may implicate him in a crime is under no legal obligation to answer. He has a constitutional right to remain silent. This right to silence is known as the *privilege against self-incrimination*. It may be invoked at all levels of governmental inquiry—in the courts, before legislative committees, at coroner's inquests, before grand juries, or when questioned by police investigators.

This privilege is an old one, having originated in England about 1650. It started out as a restriction only upon the courts—first upon the church courts (regarding heresy matters) and subsequently upon the law courts (regarding the issue of guilt or innocence to a criminal charge). About one hundred years later a related restriction was placed upon investigative agencies of government in the form of a rule of evidence that barred the use of confessions obtained by coercive interrogation tactics. Despite historical inaccuracy, the self-incrimination privilege and the confession rule are frequently looked upon as having a common origin and purpose.

Although there is no intelligent support today for an abandonment of the rule that prohibits the use as courtroom evidence of confessions extracted from accused or suspected persons by force, threats, or promises of leniency—any one of which might render a confession untrustworthy—there is much support for the abolition of the self-incrimination privilege which permits a person to refuse to testify in court or before any other governmental body conducting public hearings, without allowing that silence to be held against him.

38

The reasons given, rightly or wrongly, for the present day retention of the self-incrimination privilege are two-fold: (a) the sheer distaste for a practice whereby a person may be required by a court or other governmental body to speak out as to whether he is or is not guilty of having committed a crime; and (b) the feeling that criminal investigators should be required to use their own skills and facilities to obtain more dependable evidence than that which might be extracted from the lips of an accused or suspected person in the course of a compelled interview.

The privilege continues to be so highly regarded that a person's exercise of it cannot even be made the subject of comment at his trial. He can remain mute in court, as well as during any other form of governmental inquiry, and at trial the prosecution is precluded from making any reference to that silence. Moreover, any compelled statement will be inadmissible as evidence, and the same exclusionary rule will be applied to any other evidence that may have been obtained as a result of the leads furnished by a compelled statement.

It is general agreement that the historical origin and the policy reasons for the present day retention of the privilege support the proposition that it offers protection only against *oral* incrimination; it does not protect against the compulsory surrender of *physical* evidence.

PHYSICAL EVIDENCE LIMITATION UPON THE PRIVILEGE

Even when the evidence comes through the voice of the arrested person (or through some other act of volition), no violation of the self-incrimination privilege is involved, provided that it is to be used only for its *physical characteristics* and not for its value as *testimony*. For instance, if an arrestee is ordered to utter the words "stick 'em up", so that a robbery victim can compare his voice with that of the robber, the evidence thus obtained is considered to be of a physical nature only. The same is true of a specimen of handwriting that an arrestee may be ordered to furnish; it is solely for the purpose of a comparison between its physical characteristics and those of the document in question (e.g., a ransom note or a forged check). On the other hand, of course, an arrestee cannot be compelled to furnish a specimen of his handwriting in the form of a statement of his whereabouts at the time of the crime. Similarly, although photographs taken without consent, or over protest or resistance would be admissible, they must not be in the form of a re-enactment of the crime to which the arrestee may have confessed, because in any such re-enactment his movements might convey his thoughts and, therefore, become the equivalent of verbal expressions.

In procuring any kind of physical evidence from an accused person against his will, the police are permitted to use reasonable force —but only reasonable force. Whenever this limitation cannot be observed, the police should seek a court order for compulsory procurement.

Example

Peterson, arrested for burglary, refuses to permit his fingerprints to be taken. His hands may be held by force in such a way as to permit the necessary procedure. Fingerprints thus obtained are admissible as evidence at Peterson's trial.

Example

Smith and Jones are lawfully arrested for the possession of narcotics. Both put small plastic bags into their mouths. A police officer holds Smith's jaw and pulls out a bag. Jones, however, swallows his. Jones is taken to a hospital where, over his protests, he is given an emetic and the narcotic is recovered.

The narcotic evidence against Smith would be admitted at the trial; the narcotics evidence against Jones might be excluded—not because of a self-incrimination privilege, but upon the basis of a violation of "due process". This kind of conduct has been described as "shocking to the conscience" of the courts, and thus violative of "due process". However, some courts have held that such activities as giving emetics or using stomach pumps, if done by a physician using recognized medical techniques, are permissible.

Example

Harry, a motorist, is involved in an automobile accident. An investigating police officer suspects that Harry is intoxicated, so he takes him to a hospital where a physician is requested to extract, through a hypodermic needle, a sample of blood for the purpose of a chemical test for alcoholic intoxication. Harry refuses to consent, but the blood sample is taken anyway, over his mild resistance. The evidence may be used against him.

The following is a list of the kinds of physical evidence that may be obtained without the consent of an arrestee, by the exercise of *reasonable force* and under *reasonable circumstances,* or under other conditions upon an order of court:

"Mug" photographs
Fingerprints
Fingernail scrapings
Samples of hair
Specimens of blood, urine, or breath
Objects concealed in body cavities, including the anus or vagina

He may also be required to:

Permit the removal of clothing to be searched for concealed items such as narcotics or jewelry
Permit an inspection of his body for tattoo marks, scratches, etc.
Try on articles of clothing (e.g., a hat left at scene of crime)
Appear in a police line-up for identification purposes
Speak for purposes of voice identification by witnesses to an offense. (But if this occurs during a line-up, all the others should be required to utter the same words, rather than single out the one suspect in this manner.)
Provide specimens of his handwriting (e.g., in an extortion or kidnapping case).

EVIDENCE OBTAINED FROM INDIRECTLY COMPELLED TESTIMONY

Indirectly compelled testimony, as well as directly compelled testimony, is protected by the self-incrimination privilege. A good example of this is the case where a police officer is summoned to testify before a grand jury investigating police corruption. He is advised (1) that anything he says might be used against him in a criminal proceeding, (2) that he has the privilege of refusing to give answers that would tend to incriminate him, and (3) that, under statute and departmental rules, if he refuses to answer he would be subject to removal from office. He testifies. Then he is indicted for a criminal offense and his grand jury answers are sought to be used against him. The United States Supreme Court has held, in a situation like this, that since the officer had no choice between testifying or losing his job, he was indirectly compelled to testify, in violation of his privilege against self-incrimination. His answers to the grand jury, therefore, were not usable as evidence against him in his criminal trial.

The Supreme Court has also held that a police officer cannot be fired for refusing to sign a waiver of his self-incrimination privilege when summoned to testify before a grand jury investigating corruption in the police department. On the other hand, the Court has said that if an officer is summoned to testify before a grand jury and he refuses to answer questions *"specifically, directly, and narrowly relating to the performance of his official duties"*, the privilege against self-incrimination would be no bar to his dismissal from the police force.

Example

Captain Kidd is summoned before a grand jury investigating gambling. He is not asked to sign a waiver, although he receives the usual warning about his privilege against self-incrimination. He is then asked whether he had received money from gambler Arthur in return for overlooking Arthur's violation of the gambling laws. Kidd refuses to answer. His refusal would justify his dismissal from the force.

With respect to the present discussion of what a police officer may be compelled to do, mention should be made of the requirement that police officers submit to Polygraph ("lie-detector") examinations as part of internal police department investigations. Unless there is some legislative bar, a police officer's refusal to submit to such an examination—regarding a matter directly related to his police activities—will justify his dismissal from his position, even though it is a civil service one.

Other applications of the indirectly compelled testimony doctrine may be found in those instances where legislative efforts are made to control crime by requiring various types of registrations, licenses, or permits. For instance, the Supreme Court of the United States invalidated a federal statute that made it a criminal offense to engage in the business of gambling without first paying a federal tax, the theory being that the payer of the tax might thereby incriminate himself under state laws prohibiting gambling. To overcome this impediment of the self-incrimination privilege with respect to gun registration requirements, Congress amended the federal firearms registration act by imposing a duty upon the sellers of firearms to report the names of persons to whom guns were sold.

Forms in Which the Privilege is Available

As some of the foregoing discussion has already indicated or implied, although the self-incrimination privilege (as set forth in the Fifth Amendment to the Constitution of the United States, as well as in many state constitutions) provides that "No person shall be compelled to incriminate himself in any criminal case", it has for many years been interpreted to protect against compulsory incriminating disclosures in *any other kind of case or governmental proceeding*. This is why, as has already been stated, a witness in a legislative hearing may invoke the privilege. It is also the reason why a witness in a civil case trial may refuse to answer a question put to him that may call for an incriminating answer, or for an answer that may even "tend" to incriminate him.

Grants of Immunity

There is nothing about the self-incrimination privilege that permits a witness to refuse to answer a question that may incriminate someone else, and most certainly it affords no protection against embarrassing statements, either with regard to the witness, his wife, or any other person or institution. Also, even though a question calls for an acknowledgment that the witness committed a criminal offense, he can only invoke the privilege if the crime is one for which a prosecution is still permissible.

> *Example*
> Cole served his full sentence for robbery. In a civil suit between Jackson and Johnson or in a criminal prosecution against Foley in which the robbery issue is of some relevance, Cole may be compelled to testify about the robbery.

In view of the requirement that the incriminating statement must relate to a crime for which punishment is still possible, a court may issue a grant of immunity to a witness and thereby obtain his incriminatory testimony for use against someone else, either in the form of the witness's actual testimony at the trial of someone else, or at various investigatory hearings (grand jury, coroner's inquest), with regard to another person's guilt.

What a grant of immunity means, essentially, is that once it has been accorded a witness, whatever he says cannot be used against him in any criminal case, and it may even mean, according to a more expansive legal interpretation, that he cannot ever be prosecuted for any offense of his about which he may have had to testify. In these cases he is given what is sometimes referred to as an "immunity bath".

Once a person has been given an "immunity bath" he must testify or else he can be held in contempt of court, and a jail sentence imposed upon him. In many instances of incarceration he, figuratively speaking, "holds the key to the jail in his own hands", meaning that upon his expressed willingness to testify, he will be taken to court or before whatever investigative agency is involved, and upon giving his testimony will be released from custody.

The law varies and is in a state of some uncertainty at the present time with respect to the time a reluctant witness may be confined in jail. With respect to a grand jury hearing, or a legislative committee hearing, there are cases holding that the length of time is limited by the term of that governmental body. For matters arising in court the usual limitation for contempt is six months incarceration.

Confessions, Admissions and Exculpatory Statements

DEFINITIONS AND EXAMPLES

A *confession* is an acknowledgement of guilt; it reveals that the person making it committed a criminal offense. An *admission* is a potentially damaging statement which falls short of an acknowledgment of guilt; it may, however, give rise to an inference of guilt when considered along with other evidence. An admission is sometimes referred to as the "little brother" of a confession.

Confessions and admissions are sometimes called *inculpatory statements*. On the other hand, an *exculpatory statement* is a statement in which the maker either specifically or by inference disclaims his involvement in a criminal offense.

Example
The police suspect that Hoyt burglarized the home of Pratt. He admits that he broke into the home for the purpose of stealing something. His statement is a confession.

Example
Oaks had worked for Beard as a gardener. After the burglary of Beard's home, Oaks is questioned as a suspect. He denies he committed the burglary, but he does tell the police that on the date of the burglary he entered upon Beard's land to take a look at the condition of the garden.

Oaks's statement that he was near the house at the time of the burglary obviously does not establish that he committed the burglary. But suppose the police find out that Oaks sold a piece of jewelry to Wilson which is identified as part of the loot of the burglary. In that event Oaks's statement about being on the premises takes on real significance; it is an *admission* which permits an inference to be drawn that he was there for the purpose of committing the burglary.

Example

Barnes is questioned about the rape of Miss Kelly. He not only denies the rape but also states that he had never seen or talked to Miss Kelly. This constitutes an *exculpatory statement*.

There are occasions, of course, when even an exculpatory statement can be used against the maker. For instance, if Barnes is tried for raping Miss Kelly, the prosecution could introduce evidence that Barnes had seen and talked to Miss Kelly in a restaurant several days before the rape, thereby proving that Barnes lied about the matter, a factor which can now be considered along with all the other evidence indicative of his guilt.

At one time the legal rules governing the courtroom usage of admissions were considerably less restrictive than those applicable to confessions. For instance, a long standing prerequisite to the use of a confession in a criminal trial was a showing by the prosecution that the confession was made voluntarily, but no such showing was required for admissions. This difference no longer prevails; both types of statements must be shown to have been voluntarily given.

In addition to establishing an admission's voluntariness, the prosecution must also prove that it was preceded by the *Miranda* warnings in those instances where the maker of the statement was at that time in "custody" or "otherwise deprived of his freedom in any significant way". In such situations the same obligation would prevail with exculpatory statements.

COURTROOM PROCEDURES REGARDING STATEMENTS MADE BY ACCUSED PERSONS

A typewritten or handwritten statement bearing an accused person's handwritten name at the end does not necessarily mean that it is his signature. Nor does a label on a tape recorded statement authenticate it as being that of the accused. In all such instances no courtroom use can be made of evidence of this nature unless someone has testified, *from first-hand information,* that (a) the words or the voice sounds are, in fact, those of the accused; and (b) the recording, either in words or in sound, is an accurate reproduction of what the accused person actually said.

The trial judge, after hearing testimony in authentication, will then rule on the issue of *admissibility*. He determines whether the testimony warrants a holding that the statement is *admissible* or whether it falls short and requires a holding that it is *inadmissible*.

The mechanics for getting an accused person's statements admitted as evidence before a court or jury for its consideration (or for the consideration of both) are, briefly, as follows:

1. The police interrogator, or someone who was present when the accused person made his confession, admission, or other relevant statement, is called to the witness stand by the prosecution.

2. As soon as, or even before, there is any indication that the witness is about to reveal to a jury something the accused person said, defense counsel will object to any of the witness's testimony until a hearing has been conducted before the judge alone with regard to the admissibility of what the witness is to say—for instance: was the accused person's statement voluntary? Were the *Miranda* warnings given? The jury is then recessed while this preliminary hearing occurs.

3. The witness is then examined by the prosecutor and cross-examined by the defense. The judge himself may ask questions. In some instances the defendant may take the stand for the limited purpose of denying that he made the statement or that he made it because he was forced to do so, or that the required warnings were not given to him. By taking the stand for this purpose alone, he does not waive his privilege to remain silent about the offense itself.

4. If the trial judge decides that the statement is legally invalid, it cannot be presented to the jury nor can any reference whatsoever be made to it. If the judge concludes that the statement is a valid one, he will rule that it may be presented to the jury.

5. After the judge rules favorably for the prosecution and the jury is back in the courtroom, the prosecutor will resume his questioning of the witness, who will testify essentially that the accused made a voluntary statement after having been given the required warnings. The prosecutor will then show the witness a copy of the statement, or the tape recording if there is one, and he will be asked to state whether it is the statement of the defendant, or a recording of what he said, to which his response, of course, will be

"yes". The prosecutor may then (or later) ask the court to declare it as one of the prosecution's exhibits for jury consideration. Defense counsel will almost invariably object to the admission of the confession in evidence, and he will proceed to cross-examine the witness for the purpose of showing that the confession was improperly obtained, or that the defendant made no such statement. All this, of course, is generally repetitious of what occurred earlier while the jury was recessed, but now it is being done in the form of an attack upon the believability that the prosecution wants the jury to attach to it. In other words, after the judge has performed his function of determining *admissibility*, as a matter of law, the jurors have the responsibility of deciding whether they are to *believe* what is in the statement of facts. This means that it is up to the jury to decide what *weight* they will give to it. The prosecution, of course, wants them to believe it, whereas the defense wants them to disregard it in whole or in part.

6. Upon the conclusion of the examination and cross-examination of the authenticating witness and the judge's ruling that the confession is admissible, the prosecutor will usually proceed to read the confession to the jury, even though the jurors ordinarily will have a later opportunity, in the course of their deliberations, to examine the statement itself. If the statement is a tape recorded one, it will be played to the jury right after the authenticating witness's testimony and the ruling of the court.

The Marking as an Exhibit

A confession, as well as any other exhibit that is to be used as evidence, is first marked by the court stenographer or clerk with a number and a designation of whether it is an exhibit for the prosecution or the defense. Initially, it will bear a marking such as "State's exhibit No. 1 for identification"; or "Defendant's exhibit No. 1 for identification". Then, after the judge holds it to be admissible the "for identification" inscription is stricken out, and it becomes an official court exhibit.

There are several good reasons for the marking of exhibits. First of all, it avoids confusion, for in some cases five, ten, or perhaps even hundreds of exhibits may be involved. Next, it pinpoints for the judge and jury the object to which an attorney or a witness may be referring while talking. Then, too, and perhaps more important, when the case reaches an appellate court, which will not have the benefit of seeing and hearing the witness in person, the appellate court judges might not be able to correctly identify an unmarked object to which reference is made in the typewritten transcript of the trial court testimony. The marking practice, therefore, is not a mere technical formality; it serves a very useful practical purpose.

The Right of the Defense to a Pre-Trial Inspection of Statements Made by Accused Persons

In consideration of fairness, and as a safeguard against the conviction of an innocent person, defense counsel is accorded the right to a pre-trial inspection of any statement made by the accused to the police. By exercising this right of *discovery*, defense counsel will be in a better position to determine whatever legal defects it may contain, and he also will be better equipped to cross-examine the prosecution's witnesses and to examine his own witnesses.

In some jurisdictions, if a statement of the accused has not been written down or taped, the prosecution may be compelled to advise defense counsel, before trial, of the essential contents that are to be related at the trial.

Police Procedures in Obtaining and Recording Statements by Suspected or Accused Persons

The Miranda Rule

Mention was made earlier of the *Miranda* warnings; we now present the essential details.

In June 1966, the Supreme Court of the United States, in its five to four decision in *Miranda v. Arizona,* held that whenever a person who is about to be interrogated by a law enforcement officer *"has been taken into custody or otherwise been deprived of his freedom in any significant way",* he must be given the following warnings:

1. That he has a right to remain silent and that he need not answer any questions;

2. That if he does answer questions his answers can be used as evidence against him;

3. That he has a right to consult with a lawyer before or during the questioning by the police; and

4. That if he cannot afford to hire a lawyer one will be provided for him.

All of the warnings must be given in such a way that the suspect clearly understands what he is being told.

If the suspect indicates, at any time, or in any manner whatsoever, that he does not want to talk, the interrogation must cease. The interrogator is no longer privileged to "talk him out of" his refusal to talk.

If the suspect says, at any time, that he wants a lawyer, the interrogation must cease until he has the opportunity to confer with a lawyer, and no further questions may be asked of him outside the lawyer's presence or without the lawyer's permission. Nor can the interrogator "talk him out of" his desire for a lawyer.

In instances where the suspect requests a lawyer but cannot obtain one, and no lawyer is provided for him by the police, the interrogation must be terminated.

Under the *Miranda* decision, the only time a police interrogation can be conducted of a suspect who is in custody or otherwise restrained of his freedom in any significant way is *after* he has been given the warnings, and *after* he has expressly stated that he understands his rights, but that he is willing to answer questions without a lawyer being present. In other words, the suspect may waive his *Miranda* rights, but the waiver must be a "knowing and explicit" one.

Example

Sergeant Jones is on duty as desk sergeant in the precinct house. Sidney rushes in and says to Sergeant Jones: "I just shot my wife". Sergeant Jones asks "Where is she?" Sidney says "2647 Mariposa Street, Apt. 4G". A patrol car and an ambulance are immediately dispatched to that address.

Both statements would be admissible as evidence at Sidney's trial for shooting his wife, because Sidney volunteered the information, without having been interrogated at all; and because the sergeant had both a right and duty to find out where the victim was in order to get aid to her as soon as possible.

But Sergeant Jones now says "Where is the gun?" Sidney replies: "I threw it into a sewer behind the house". This statement would be inadmissible because the *Miranda* warnings had not been given.

Although Sergeant Jones had not formally placed Sidney under arrest it is clear that he would not have let Sidney leave if he had expressed a desire to do so. Therefore, the situation becomes a custodial one and the *Miranda* warnings are required before there is any further questioning.

Moreover, if the police had gone to the house and found the gun in the sewer, the *gun itself* would be inadmissible because it was the "fruit of the poisonous tree"; that is, the finding of the gun was a product of an inadmissible statement.

After Sidney's initial volunteered statement (sometimes referred to as a "threshold" statement), Jones should have advised him of his rights as soon as he had dispatched assistance to the wife.

Example

Mrs. Craig is arrested for the killing of her husband. Before she is interrogated she is told that she has a right to remain silent and a right to a lawyer. She said she did not want a lawyer and was willing to talk anyway. She proceeds to tell how and why she killed her husband.

The confession is inadmissible, due to the fact that she was not also told that anything she said could be used against her and that if she could not afford a lawyer one would be supplied her free.

(The foregoing example illustrates the extensive nature of the *Miranda* requirements; in other words, if any one of the four elements is omitted, a confession becomes a nullity.)

Example

Miss Bunch is arrested for larceny. Before she is interrogated she is given the *Miranda* warnings. She announces she wants a lawyer. The interrogator says: "Why do you need a lawyer, if you're telling the truth? Why go to the expense and delay this whole matter?" Thereafter, she confesses.

The confession is invalid. The interrogator had no right to "talk her out of" her desire for a lawyer.

Once the *Miranda* warnings have been given and a valid waiver has been obtained from a suspect, a police interrogator may proceed to interrogate him, if, in doing so, there is no violation of the statutory or court rule prohibiting an "unnecessary delay" in taking the individual to a judge or other judicial magistrate. In interpreting the meaning of "unnecessary delay", the state courts have given the police much more leeway than have the federal courts.

Even after the *Miranda* warnings are given, and even after a valid waiver has been obtained from the suspect, the police interrogator will be faced with still another issue: what interrogation tactics and techniques are permissible in an effort to ascertain whether the suspect is telling the truth, or in an effort to obtain a confession from him if he is guilty?

Until the courts or the legislatures become more specific as to what is or is not permissible, we suggest that the police interrogator rely upon the following guideline with regard to the tactics and techniques he may use, by asking himself: "*Is what I am about to do, or say, likely to make an innocent person confess?*"

If a fair answer to the question is "no", the interrogator should go ahead and do or say what was contemplated; on the other hand, if the answer is "yes", he should refrain from doing or saying what he had in mind.

Example

Police interrogator Case tells Vinton, a suspect in the killing of his wife, that anybody, including Case himself, who had been treated by a wife as Vinton had been, might have done the same thing. He is further told that he will feel better inside once he gets this thing off his chest. He confesses.

Since what Vinton was told is not likely to make an innocent man confess, his confession is admissible as evidence.

Example

Galvin, who served time for selling narcotics, is questioned about a forcible rape. He is told that the victim has identified him, but that if he confesses the prosecution will only charge him with an assault and battery. Galvin confesses.

The confession is invalid. Confronted with the victim's identification, and being handicapped by his criminal record, which could be used to attack his credibility if he takes the witness stand, Galvin, even if innocent, might confess. To him, going to jail on a minor charge would be preferable to risking a penitentiary sentence for rape.

Example

Thomas is being questioned about a burglary. He denies he committed the offense. His interrogator then says: "We also believe your wife was in on the burglary; unless you tell the truth we'll lock her up too." Thomas says: "What will happen to our infant daughter if you do that?" Response: "You should have thought of that before you and your wife pulled off that job." Thomas confesses.

It is conceivable that an innocent man might confess a crime to avoid the kind of consequence of a continued denial of guilt, and therefore such a confession would be held invalid.

A confession obtained without having first given the *Miranda* warnings, or an involuntary confession obtained by the use of force, threats, or promises of leniency cannot be used in the presentation of the prosecution's case. In a 1971 United States Supreme Court decision, however, the Court did allow a limited use by the prosecution of a confession obtained without being preceded by the *Miranda* warnings. It held that such a confession may be used to attack the credibility of the confessor (that is, "impeach" him) if he takes the witness stand in his own defense and denies that he committed the offense for which he is on trial.

Example

A police interrogator forgets to give two of the four required *Miranda* warnings to kidnapping suspect Davis. He confesses. At his trial, however, he takes the witness stand in his own defense and denies his guilt.

In attacking the truthfulness of the defendant's testimony, the prosecution can use the confession, despite the fact that it could not have been used if the defendant had declined to take the witness stand in his own behalf.

Example

Officer Phillips arrested Williams on a warrant for the rape of Carry Nation. He takes Williams to the detective bureau where Detective McNulty, mistakenly, but in good faith, believes that Officer Phillips had given Williams the *Miranda* warnings, and he immediately proceeds to interrogate Williams. McNulty asks: "Did you rape Carry Nation?" Williams replies: "You mean that skinny red head that works at the Shamrock Bar? I wouldn't waste my time with her."

In Williams's trial for rape, his statements to McNulty could not be used as part of the prosecution's case in chief, because the *Miranda* warnings had not been given to Williams and Detective McNulty's good faith mistake is no excuse. (This illustrates an important point: do not *assume* that someone else has advised a suspect. If you do not *know* for a fact that he has been given the warnings, give them yourself.)

Assume, however, that in his own defense Williams takes the witness stand and says that he has never heard of Carry

Nation. At this point Williams' statement to McNulty could be used to prove that he did know who Carry Nation was and that he is now lying about never having heard of her.

Even though a *Miranda*-defective confession can be used for impeachment purposes, the same does not hold true with regard to an involuntary confession. The obvious difference between that kind of confession and one obtained without the *Miranda* warnings is the factor of trustworthiness; a non-Miranda-warning confession may nevertheless be absolutely true, whereas one obtained by force, threats or promises may well be false.

The Future of the Miranda Rule

We have already commented upon a Supreme Court inroad upon the *Miranda* rule—the use of a non-Miranda warning confession for impeachment purposes. There has also been a more basic legislative one—an effort to completely nullify the *Miranda* rule.

In the Omnibus Crime Control and Safe Streets Act of 1968, Congress decreed that the absence of warnings of constitutional rights would not render a confession inadmissible in federal cases, and that the test of confession admissibility shall be the conventional one of voluntariness. Although the lack of warnings might be considered by a court or jury in determining whether a confession was voluntary, the act provides that that fact alone would not categorically ban the use of the confession as evidence of guilt, as is now the decision law under *Miranda*.

When a case involving the constitutional validity of this provision of the Omnibus Crime Act reaches the Supreme Court, the Court will be faced with the issue of overruling the *Miranda* case, which held, of course, that the warnings therein prescribed were constitutionally required. In other words, if something is unconstitutional, then Congress is without authority to validate it; that being so, about the only way, strictly speaking, that the Court can sustain the validity of the foregoing provision is to overrule *Miranda*—a not unreasonable expectation in view of changes occurring in the composition of the Court and the fact that the five to four decision in *Miranda* itself had overruled two of the Court's own cases which had been decided only a few years prior to *Miranda*.

A word of caution, however: since there is a possibility that the Supreme Court may hold that the foregoing enactment is unconstitutional, it is advisable for federal interrogators to continue to follow the *Miranda* mandate until there is a decision that settles the issue regarding the recent act of Congress. A case will undoubtedly reach the Court before long, perhaps one in which one or more of the warnings may have been inadvertently omitted, or where the omission may have been deliberate in order to present a test case to the Court. Until then, however, it would be unwise to jeopardize the validity of a large number of confessions that the prosecution may need in presenting its case-in-chief and not simply for impeachment purposes alone.

It should also be remembered that the Congressional Act applies only to federal cases; it does not apply on the state level, so state officers are still bound by the *Miranda* decision.

The McNabb-Mallory Rule

For many years a rule existed in the federal courts that if there was an unnecessary delay—even for an hour or so—in bringing an arrested person before a judge or federal commissioner for the placing of formal charges against him, a confession obtained from him during the period of delay would not be usable as evidence at his trial. The rule was first laid down in the 1943 case of *McNabb v. United States* and then reiterated in *Mallory v. United States*, 1957. It was promulgated by the Supreme Court of the United States in the exercise of its supervisory power over lower federal courts.

Since the McNabb-Mallory rule was not based upon constitutional due process considerations, or upon any other provision of the Bill of Rights, the rule was not binding upon the states. Of all the state courts only the Supreme Courts of Michigan and Delaware were inclined to adopt a similar rule, but they eventually abandoned the idea and returned to the conventional confession admissibility test of voluntariness. The rule persisted within the federal system, however, until 1968. In that year Congress, in the Omnibus Crime Control and Safe Streets Act, abolished it. This Congress was clearly privileged to do since the rule was not one of constitutional dimensions.

With the abandonment of the McNabb-Mallory rule in the federal system, it is unlikely that any state courts or legislatures will ever adopt it on their own initiative.

The Effect of Interrogation Trickery and Deceit

In a number of confession cases decided by the Supreme Court of the United States during the past several years, mention was sometimes made in derogatory terms to the use of interrogation tactics and techniques based upon trickery and deceit. In the *Miranda* decision itself, the Court castigated some writers, including one of the present authors (Inbau), for their recommendation of such tactics and techniques. This caused a number of legal scholars to assume that upon some future occasion the Court would reverse a confession case for that reason alone. But the assumption was invalidated, however, in an April 1969 decision of the Supreme Court in *Frazier v. Cupp*. In the *Frazier* case the defendant, while being questioned as a murder suspect, was told falsely that a suspected accomplice had confessed. In its opinion affirming the confession, the Court (through Justice Thurgood Marshall) said:

> The fact that the police misrepresented the statements that [the suspected accomplice] had made is, while relevant, insufficient in our view to make this otherwise voluntary confession inadmissible. These cases must be decided by viewing the 'totality of the circumstances. . .'

Police interrogators may very rightly derive considerable comfort from this decision and from what the Court said, because the technique of "playing one suspect against the other" is actually one of the most blatant pieces of interrogation trickery; consequently, with the toleration of its usage by the Court, there should be no difficulty with respect to other less objectionable tactics and techniques. Moreover, this case decision may very well evidence a final realization on the part of most members of the Court that there is an intrinsic and unavoidable element of trickery and deceit in almost all interrogations of suspected persons. Very few interrogations are ever conducted for the benefit of the accused; their primary purpose is to ascertain the truth, which may well place the suspect in a penitentiary. Consequently, unless the suspect is told at the outset that the interrogator is seeking to "get the goods on him" and that for his own welfare perhaps he should say nothing, practically all confessions would have to be voided because of interrogation trickery and deceit.

THE RECORDING OF A CONFESSION

After a suspect has made an oral confession, what else, if anything, must the interrogator do in anticipation of a criminal prosecution and the admissibility of the confession as evidence?

First of all, the interrogator should know that (except in Texas) an oral confession is just as admissible in evidence as a written one; the only difference is that a written or otherwise recorded and acknowledged one is more likely to be believed. It is suggested, therefore, that if there is to be reliance upon the oral confession alone some one or more persons in addition to the interrogator should hear it. In consequence, more than one witness would be available to establish that it was indeed made.

Provided that the law of the particular jurisdiction permits a secret sound recording of such interviews, or if consent of the suspect had previously been obtained, a recording may have already been made of everything the suspect said. In that event, of course, either all or the essential parts of the recording may be usable as evidence at the trial.

In the absence of a sound recording or video taping of the entire interrogation, one may be made of merely the confession; or the oral confession could be reduced to writing. The latter form is the preferred one, for a number of practical considerations, the foremost of which is the relative simplicity of its courtroom presentation.

In pursuance of the written form procedure, the usual practice, after an oral confession has been made, is to have a stenographer present to record, in shorthand or by stenotype, the questions asked by the interrogator and the answers given by the confessor. Thereafter, the typewritten transcript of such a recording should be shown, as well as read, to the confessor, after which he should be requested to sign it. (The details of this procedure, and the precautions to be followed, are presented in *Criminal Interrogation and Confession* (2d ed. 1967) by Fred E. Inbau and John E. Reid.)

Even when a written confession bears the signed name of the confessor, at the time of trial the prosecution must prove (a) that it bears the confessor's signature, and (b) that it accurately represents what the confessor said. Along with this, of course, there must be testimony as to the voluntariness of the confession and as to other legally prescribed prerequisites.

The Multiple Offense Confession

If the confessor has confessed to the commission of another, or other, unrelated offenses (for example, several different robberies), separate confessions should be taken of each one. This is necessary because of an evidentiary rule, or perhaps even a constitutionally required one, that prohibits the use of evidence in a criminal case merely to show that the accused is a bad fellow, from which a jury may infer that if he is such a bad fellow he must have committed the offense for which he is now on trial, an obviously unfair inference.

There are some cases, however, in which it is practically impossible to avoid including in a confession to one crime references to certain other ones. In such instances the references will not destroy the confession's validity.

> *Example*
>   Baldwin is charged with the rape of a woman in her own home. According to what he told the police, the initial purpose of entering the home was to commit a burglary and that the rape was an afterthought. He also admits that, as he was leaving, the rape victim's husband returned home, whereupon Baldwin hit him over the head and took his wallet.

The facts are all so closely related in time and place as to render it practically impossible to describe the offense of rape in the confession, or present the evidence in support of the rape charge in court, without going into the explanation of the reason for being in the home (burglary) or without having the husband describe the circumstances under which he observed the defendant. Because of the practicalities of the situation, the evidence of the two other offenses may be offered at the trial on the rape charge.

There are other exceptions also, as when the inclusion of references to other crimes is for a definitely legitimate and necessary purpose; for instance, to establish the defendant's intent, motive, or lack of mistake with regard to the act for which he is on trial. In a later part of this book, we will discuss various exceptions.

A good rule for interrogators to follow in taking confessions is this: whenever multiple offenses are involved, confessions should be taken, whenever practically possible, of each one; and in any one confession there should be no references to other unrelated offenses or misdeeds.

THE MULTIPLE OFFENDER CONFESSION

Where two or more persons have committed an offense, the confession of any one of them is admissible only against him. As to any of the others referred to in the confession, it is hearsay and not usable as evidence against them. Consequently, a difficult problem confronts a prosecutor who has in his files a confession from one or more of the offenders, but not from all of them, and all of them, including the confessors, are pleading "not guilty." But there is very little the interrogator can do except to try his best to obtain confessions from all. Lacking such success he will necessarily have to let stand the references by a confessor to the part played by his accomplices in the commission of the crime.

CORROBORATING THE CONFESSION

The conclusion of a successful interrogation and the recording of the confession is not the end of responsibility for the police. They should check into every aspect of the confession, and to such an extent that in many instances the evidence thereby secured will in and of itself furnish proof of guilt beyond a reasonable doubt, thus obviating the need to use the actual confession, or perhaps only for impeaching the accused in the event he testifies in his own behalf and denies he committed the offense.

Substantiating evidence should always be sought and made known to the prosecutor. For instance, in a murder case, if the confessor states that after he stabbed the victim he went to a gas station washroom to wash the blood off his hand, the police should go to that station and search for confirmatory evidence. If blood is found there, on a towel, perhaps, it should be preserved as evidence. Also, gas station attendants should be questioned as to whether they saw someone come in with blood on his hands, or whether anyone fitting the confessor's description had been seen there at the time in question; if so, their statements to that effect should be reduced to writing and signed by them. All of this follow-up can be extremely helpful to the prosecution. Such thoroughness will also reflect credit upon the investigators and their department.

A number of interrogators follow the practice of taking several color photographs of the confessor soon after his confession as a safeguard against possible later accusations of interrogation brutality. Such photographs, consisting of front, back and side views of the confessor, are admissible in evidence for the purpose of rebutting any such false accusations.

Section 11

Eyewitness and Voice Identification Evidence

Of all the types of evidence that the courts have accepted over the years, one of the least reliable has been eyewitness and voice identifications, particularly the latter.

The time may come when "voice print" instrumentation and techniques will add validity to voice identification in those instances where a print can be made of the voice of the criminal offender, as when a kidnap ransom is demanded over the telephone, and a comparison made between it and a specimen that has been recorded of the suspect's voice, but what human testimonial evidence is now available leaves much to be desired. Regrettably, nothing of similar scientific assistance seems in the offing with respect to the improvement of eyewitness identifications. Human fallibility is an extremely important factor.

Because of the basic weakness in eyewitness identifications, the Supreme Court of the United States decided several years ago that certain precautions had to be followed by the police whenever they wanted crime victims or witnesses to view suspects produced by the police. Two basic rules evolved. First, a "line-up" rather than a "show-up" had to be conducted; in other words, several persons who generally fitted the description given by the victim or witness had to be presented rather than merely the suspect himself. Second, to insure that even the line-up itself would be a fair one, and that no encouraging suggestions would be offered to the viewing crime witnesses, a lawyer must be present at the line-up unless the suspect waives his right to have a lawyer present, after first being advised of that right.

61

With regard to the lawyer's presence at the line-up (as an observer only, since he is not to ask questions or give directions), the Supreme Court left the door open for some alternative procedure—perhaps a sound movie of the proceeding, which would permit an evaluation to be made of it at a later date in advance of trial.

Without such precautions being taken, an identifying witness will not be permitted to testify about the line-up at which the defendant was "fingered", or even to make an in-court identification of the defendant unless the prosecution can establish that what happened at the police station did not "taint" (that is, influence) the in-court identification. What this means, then, is that the prosecution must show that the victim or other witness got such a good look at the offender at the scene of the crime that the happening at the police station had no effect on the validity of the courtroom identification. But this may be a difficult task for the prosecution in many instances.

Example

Burry is walking home on a fairly dark street one night. He is jumped from behind, thrown to the ground, and his wallet taken. Burry only caught a fleeting glimpse of the robber's face.

Carter is arrested. The police place him in a line-up, but without first advising him that he had a right to have a lawyer present. Moreover, no lawyer was present. Burry fingers Carter as the robber.

At Carter's trial, Burry would not be permitted to testify that he had identified Carter in the line-up because an attorney was not present. Moreover, Burry probably would not even be permitted to make an in-court identification, because the rather unsatisfactory view Burry had of the robber at the time of the crime would make it very difficult for the prosecution to establish that the improper police station identification had not tainted the courtroom identification.

Example

Mrs. Ryan, a clerk in a well lighted store, was robbed by an unmasked bandit who remained in the store for about three minutes as he gathered up his loot. Lawless was arrested for the robbery, placed in a line-up without benefit of a lawyer's presence, and fingered by Mrs. Ryan.

Mrs. Ryan would not be permitted to testify about the line-up identification, but, because of the favorable opportunity she had to get a good look at the robber, the prosecution may be able to use her in-court identification anyway. The prosecution could establish that the courtroom identification was unaffected by the earlier one in the police station.

Example

Turner was robbed. He described his assailant as male, white, about 5' 4", slight build, wearing a "tee" shirt and khaki trousers. Van Pelt, who fits this description, is arrested and placed in a line-up.

Because there were no jail inmates available for line-up purposes at the time, O'Houlihan, the investigating detective, asked five of his fellow officers to stand in the line-up with Van Pelt. Only one of the officers selected was in uniform, but the other four were all large men over six feet in height and wearing suits. Van Pelt's attorney was present at the line-up but said nothing (nor is he privileged to say or do anything but observe). Turner picks Van Pelt out as the robber.

Under these circumstances, it is likely that the line-up would be considered "tainted" even though Turner's attorney was present. The dissimilarities between Van Pelt and the others in the line-up were so great that, in effect, Van Pelt was "singled out" for Turner to identify. Thus, if a line-up is fundamentally unfair, the "due process" right of a suspect may be violated even though his attorney is present.

The Supreme Court has made some allowance regarding the line-up-lawyer requirements in emergency circumstances.

Example

Mr. and Mrs. Burns are being robbed. Burns tries to take the robber's gun away from him, but is killed in the process. The robber then shoots Mrs. Burns.

Mrs. Burns is taken to a hospital in serious condition. Soon thereafter, the police arrest a suspect, Larry, and they bring him to the hospital to be viewed by Mrs. Burns. She identifies him.

Under these circumstances the viewing of Burns alone would not prevent a subsequent in-court identification.

Under a recently developed legal principle in some jurisdictions, it is now possible, in those cases where probable cause (reasonable grounds) is lacking for an actual arrest, to obtain a court order requiring a person, whom the police only *reasonably suspect*, to ap-

pear at a police station to participate in a line-up. (He would be entitled, of course, to have counsel present.)

Example

A young lady is raped while visiting in the home of a
relative. Her description of the rapist generally fits that of a
young man who lives several blocks away, but had not previously been seen by the victim. A court order may issue requiring him to appear in a line-up, and to even utter the
words spoken by the rapist, for voice identification purposes.

Section 12

Opinion Evidence — Lay and Expert

There is a general rule of evidence that witnesses can only testify to what they observed; in other words, they can only relate facts, and not the inferences they drew from those facts. Stated another way, witnesses are not to express *opinions*. The legal system allows only the trial judge, or the jury, to indulge in inferences.

> *Example*
> Foster witnesses an accident in which a pedestrian was hit by an automobile at a street intersection. Foster may testify that the traffic signal was green for the path of the automobile but red for the pedestrian. He could not testify, however, that the pedestrian was walking "recklessly" or that the motorist was driving "carefully".

As with practically all evidentiary rules, there are certain exceptions to this one.

LAY WITNESS OPINION

A *lay witness* may express an opinion in describing what he observed if that is the only feasible way he can impart anything of value to the judge or jury.

> *Example*
> In a murder case in which the defendant contends he killed in self-defense, a witness may testify that the victim approached the defendant in a "menacing manner".

65

Example

In a hit-and-run pedestrian killing, a witness may testify that the car was travelling at a "high rate of speed", or about 70 mph.

Example

After witnessing an automobile-pedestrian accident, Neal sees the driver get out of the car and walk up to the pedestrian. Neal is also close enough to smell the driver's breath.

At the driver's trial, Neal may testify that the driver "staggered" toward the pedestrian, that there was the odor of whiskey on the driver's breath, and that in Neal's opinion the driver was intoxicated.

Expert Opinion

Opinion evidence may be given by a witness who possesses a special skill with regard to a science, art, profession, business or occupation that is beyond the capacity of the average layman (in other words, the jury). The reason for this is that if such a witness—referred to as an *expert*—were confined to merely stating what he observed to the jury, as well as to the average judge, they would not be helped very much, or perhaps not at all. They would not be able to know what significance to attach to those observations. Consequently, the courts will permit an expert to relate not only what he observed but also to express an *opinion* as to what those facts mean.

Example

A partially burned dead body is removed from a fire scene. A forensic pathologist performs an autopsy and conducts various chemical tests. He finds no evidence of carbon monoxide in the victim's respiratory system, nor in the blood stream, but he does find a fracture of the hyoid bone ("Adam's apple") in the neck. To a layman these two facts may not mean much. To the forensic pathologist, however, they mean that the victim was dead because of causes other than smoke and fire. They signify suffocation by means of strangulation. He may so testify at a trial of a person charged with the criminal homicide.

Although an expert is accorded the privilege of expressing an opinion, there is one limitation imposed by some courts: he must stop short of settling "the ultimate issue" in the case.

Example

Elizabeth, the wife of Edwards, is charged with murdering him. She told the police that Edwards had threatened to shoot her but in a scuffle the fatal shot was fired when the pistol was close to his body.

From a study of the area of the wound, a firearms expert may testify that because of the absence of powder residues around the wound, the weapon, in his opinion, was fired from a distance not less than two feet away. However, he may not testify that in his opinion Elizabeth fired the shot.

Example

In the trial of Speckman for murdering eight nurses in their townhouse apartment, a fingerprint expert testified that in his opinion latent fingerprints found on the door of the townhouse were Speckman's. The expert could testify that Speckman had been in the townhouse *at some time*, but he could not testify that Speckman killed the nurses.

An expert must be *qualified,* as such; that is, the judge must be satisfied that he is in fact an expert and possesses those special skills and knowledge which will make his opinion of value to the jurors. This is usually accomplished by the party calling the expert witness to the stand and examining him as to his credentials. Thus the expert witness may be asked to tell about his academic training, including advanced degrees and special schools attended, how long he has been engaged in his particular specialty, honors and awards received, books and papers that he had read or written in his field, and any other facts pointing toward his expertise. The opposing attorney may then cross-examine the witness in order to demonstrate any "weaknesses" in his expertise. The judge then makes a ruling as to whether the witness will be accepted as an expert. On occasion, if the purported expert is nationally known, or is known by the opposing party to be an expert, his credentials as such may be conceded, although usually the attorney who called the witness (e.g., the D.A.) will nevertheless, for the benefit of the jury, bring out information bearing on his expert qualifications.

While it is true that expert witnesses are often professional specialists such as doctors, scientists, criminalists and engineers, quite often a police officer who specializes in a certain area of law enforcement may be qualified to give an expert opinion.

Example

Sergeant Metros, of the Vice Bureau of a police department, takes the witness stand. He testifies, upon questioning by the prosecutor, that he has been assigned to the Narcotics Squad for 5 years, that he has been to several law enforcement schools dealing with narcotics, that he has made some 500 narcotics arrests and searches, and that he has had the opportunity to smell burning marijuana on numerous occasions. With these facts in evidence, the judge would let him express his opinion as an expert that in the case in which he is testifying, the odor which he smelled coming from the defendant's apartment was in his opinion that of burning marijuana.

Likewise, a detective of similar experience in gambling cases would be able to testify that in his opinion certain writings were bet slips, and an experienced prostitution detective could state his expert opinion that certain listings of names, addresses and symbols found in a house of prostitution were "trick books" or names of clients. In addition, trained and experienced traffic officers are often qualified as experts with regard to their opinion in traffic accident cases such as how fast the cars were going at the time of impact, based upon their interpretation of skid marks. Of course, in all of these cases the judge would have to be satisfied that the officer was, in fact, an expert.

Maps, Diagrams, Sketches, Models and Photographs

Courtroom use is frequently made of maps, diagrams, sketches, models and photographs of crime scenes and dead bodies or other objects of relevance in a criminal prosecution.

Contrary to what is generally believed, evidence of this nature may be used even without the appearance on the witness stand of the persons or person who prepared the exhibits. All that is required is for someone—a *sponsoring witness*—to testify that he has seen or is otherwise familiar with what is shown by the exhibit and that it is a *true and accurate representation of what it purports to show.*

Example

Norman, a motorist, is prosecuted for reckless homicide arising out of the killing of a pedestrian at the intersection of Main and First Street. Witness Smith, who lives near the intersection, testifies that the victim was three-quarters of the way across the intersection when struck by Norman's car. The prosecutor wants Smith to point out, on a map, diagram or sketch of the intersection precisely where the pedestrian was at the impact. Such an exhibit is usable after Smith first testifies that he is familiar with the intersection and the exhibit truly and accurately portrays the scene. There is no need to authenticate the exhibit by the person who actually prepared it.

Example

A murder is committed in a home. In preparation for trial the prosecutor had someone prepare a scale model of the en-

69

tire house. The homeowner or someone else familiar with the house may testify as to the model's correctness and thereafter any witness may refer to the model during the course of his testimony.

Example

A photograph is made of a room in which an altercation occurred that resulted in the death of one of the participants as he fell and hit his head on a radiator. The photograph, which shows the victim and the disarrayed furniture, can be used as evidence without the need of having it authenticated by the photographer himself. All that is required is for a witness at the scene to testify that what he observed is truly and correctly shown in the photograph.

Some courts, but not all, allow in evidence a photograph of a reconstructed crime scene, but the better police practice is to record the original scene photographically. Where they have failed to do so, however, an effort may be made to rectify the error by rearranging the objects in the scene (for instance, chairs and tables) at the direction of a witness and then make a photograph of it.

X-Rays

A more stringent rule applies to an x-ray than to a photograph, for the simple reason that in many instances there is no one who can say that he saw with his own eyes what the x-ray itself discloses. Consequently, the x-ray technician, or the physician under whose direction it was taken, must appear as a witness to: (a) identify the x-ray (in other words, that it is the x-ray of a particular body part, or object); and (b) to testify that the instrument used was a standard one and in good working order.

Color Photographs

In some instances a color photograph will show something much better than a black-and-white one. Where that is the situation the color photograph may be used in evidence even though it may disclose more vividly the horror of what occurred. On the other hand if its *prejudicial effect* outweighs its *probative value* it is inadmissible.

Example

Pete is murdered by strangulation. A forensic pathologist or one of his assistants takes a color photograph to show the fracture of the "Adam's apple" in the victim's neck, which fracture would be barely visible in a black and white photograph. Although blood shows in the picture it is nevertheless admissible because its probative value outweighs its prejudicial effect.

Example

In the foregoing case the prosecution also offers in evidence a color photograph which merely shows the body cavity after having been cut open at autopsy by the forensic pathologist.

It would be reversible error for a trial judge to admit this photograph in evidence; it is of little or no probative value and could only serve the purpose of inflaming the jury.

Section 14

Scientific Evidence

The results of examinations, tests and experiments by men of science are admissible in evidence provided the results stem from techniques or procedures that are accepted by the particular field of science in which they fall, or by a specialty within that field.

Example

Medical examiner Dr. Petty made an examination of a dead body found in an automobile parked in a garage. To his trained eyes the color of the skin indicated death due to carbon monoxide fumes. He performed an autopsy and conducted toxicological tests which revealed traces of carbon monoxide in the blood. He observed no wounds, externally or internally, and no other cause of death indications such as a coronary attack.

Dr. Petty may testify that in his opinion death was due to carbon monoxide poisoning, because the techniques and tests he employed and the deductions he made from his observations are generally recognized as valid by the medical profession, and especially so within the pathology specialty.

Example

A fingerprint expert compares a developed latent fingerprint left at the scene of a crime with an inked fingerprint impression made by a suspect's finger. He concludes that both fingerprint impressions were made by the same person.

The expert's opinion is admissible because there is a general acceptance among fingerprint experts and by a substantial body of scientific men generally of the individuality of fingerprints.

Example

Manson is involved in a motor vehicle accident. A specimen of his breath is obtained and a test is made of it to determine whether it contains any alcohol, and if so, how much.

The results of the test reveal that the alcohol in the blood was .19 percent. A person trained in such testing and evaluation may testify that Manson was in a state of intoxication.

Chemical tests for intoxication are generally accepted within the medical profession and also among toxicologists, whether they are doctors of medicine or not. Moreover, at the present time, because of this widespread scientific recognition, the various legislatures have placed the stamp of approval on such testing and test results. Most states have also enacted laws that permit the revocation or suspension of the license of a motorist who refuses, after an arrest, to submit to a chemical test for alcoholic intoxication.

Example

Clifton is arrested for speeding. The evidence against him consists of the indicators on an electronic speed meter or radar device. Courts readily accept such evidence because the reliability of the instrument, and the scientific basis upon which it rests, have been generally accepted as valid.

Example

Olson is suspected of sending kidnapping ransom notes, some of which were handwritten and some typed. Specimens are obtained of Olson's handwriting from letters and other documents he had written, and also by means of having him write out the dictated contents of the handwritten ransom notes. Specimens are also obtained of the type from his typewriter.

Mr. Doud, a professional document examiner, compares the various writings and concludes therefrom that Olson wrote the handwritten ransom notes and that his typewriter had been used to prepare the typewritten notes.

Mr. Doud's opinion is admissible in evidence because the validity of such examinations is generally accepted as producing reliable indications of the source of such writings as the ransom notes.

Example

A Polygraph or so-called "lie detector" test is conducted upon a criminal suspect. The examiner concludes that the suspect is lying when he denies committing the offense.

In the absence of an agreement between the suspect, his attorney and the prosecutor, prior to the test, to permit the results to be used as evidence, the opinion of the examiner is not admissible in court. The polygraph technique is not as yet accepted in the general field of science, nor in any particular recognized branch of it. (An argument has been advanced, however, that the group evaluation which should be considered is that of the polygraph examiners themselves.)

Example

Cartin is suspected of shooting Foy. Paraffin is spread over his appropriate hand and the cast is chemically tested with a solution of diphenylamine in concentrated sulphuric acid in an effort to determine whether it contains any powder residues.

Although highly acclaimed initially, this test has not been generally accepted among chemists or firearms experts because scientific tests have shown that a number of other substances that may have innocently come upon a person's hands may produce a chemical reaction the same as that occasioned by powder residues.

Since the diphenylamine test lacks scientific approval, the results are inadmissible as evidence. (We should note, however, that more recent tests involving the use of other chemicals and techniques offer considerable encouragement for ultimate scientific approval and judicial acceptance.)

Obtaining the Evidence for Scientific Testing

One matter of considerable importance regarding scientific evidence involves the procedures to be followed in obtaining specimens of fingerprints, fingernail scrapings, hair specimens, and other physical evidence from the body of suspected persons. With a consenting suspect no problem is presented beyond the need for securing adequate samplings and preserving them in a proper manner for presentation to the expert who is to make the scientific tests. Problems do arise, however, when a suspected or arrested person refuses to give up such evidence, and when the police anticipate refusal on the part of a person against whom there exists less than probable cause to effect a lawful arrest.

As previously discussed, a lawfully *arrested* person must submit to the procurement of *physical* specimens sought for scientific tests. His self-incrimination privilege affords him no protection. In fact, the only insulation he has is the prohibition against the police use of procurement procedures of a highly offensive nature, in violation of constitutional "due process". Until recently there seemed to be no way by which the police could secure physical evidence from a person against whom probable cause was lacking for a lawful arrest —in other words, from a person whom the police merely looked upon as a *suspect* rather than as the probable offender. Consider this case, as an example. A popular young girl is found dead in her apartment, the result of manual strangulation. On a nearby table are two glasses and some empty beer bottles. Her fingerprints are found on one of the glasses. Some other person's fingerprints are on the other glass and on the beer bottles. Good investigative procedures would warrant a checking of the unidentified prints with those of some of her male suitors, of which we shall assume there are five. The prints of three of them are already on file, but a comparison with them results in their elimination. What, then, about the other two friends of the deceased whose prints are not on file. Without any evidence indicative of probable guilt other than mere suspicion, an arrest of either or both of them would be unlawful and fingerprint specimens taken from them could not be used as evidence. But, in some jurisdictions, a legal procedure is now available for securing the desired evidence—a request for a court order requiring that the two remaining male friends submit to the taking of their fingerprints without their being placed under arrest. A similar order could be issued for the procurement of any other type of physical evidence from persons against whom there is a fair measure of suspicion of guilt, as in the foregoing situation.

Section 15

Accomplice Testimony and the Confession of an Accomplice

When an offense is committed by two or more persons acting in concert, and one of them admits his guilt and is willing to testify against the other one or more offenders (in other words, he "turns state's evidence"), there is no legal obstacle to the prosecution's use of him as a *witness*. He will thereby "confront" the accused and he will also be subject to cross-examination, so there can be no objection on the basis of "hearsay".

> *Example*
> Albert, Bernard, and Collin are on trial for robbery. Collin takes the witness stand and tells how the three of them committed the crime. This is permissible because the attorneys for Albert and Bernard have the opportunity to cross-examine Collin in order to "shake" his story or to cast doubt on his testimony.

On the other hand, however, a *confession* of an accomplice cannot be used as evidence against any of the others; with respect to them it would be "hearsay".

In former times, where two or more persons were tried together, and only one, or more, but not all, had confessed, the confession of one could be used, provided the trial judge instructed the jury to consider it only against the confessor and not as evidence against the non-confessing defendants. In a further effort toward that end, the names mentioned in the confession might have been blocked out, so references would be to *A*, or *B*, or *C*, etc., although not much imagination would have to be exercised to figure out who

76

they were. At any rate, in 1969, the Supreme Court of the United States held that these efforts were inadequate as safeguards against the rights of nonconfessing co-defendants. As a consequence, the prosecution now has to try the confessor separately from the others, or else, if they are all tried together, the prosecution must refrain from using the confession as evidence.

Example

Childs, Young, and Olds are arrested for murder. Childs confesses, but later retracts his confession and enters a plea of "not guilty".

If the prosecution wishes to use Childs's confession, he must be tried alone; at a trial of all three the confession could not be used even if the judge were to tell the jury to consider it against Childs alone.

CORROBORATION REQUIREMENT

Whenever an accomplice "turns state's evidence" and testifies for the prosecution, a rule applies which requires the trial judge to caution the jury to consider carefully the accomplice's possible motivation to lie (in return for the state's promise not to prosecute him). Another rule is that an accomplice's testimony must be corroborated by other evidence. In other words, a conviction cannot stand on an accomplice's testimony alone; other evidence must give credibility to it.

Section 16

Evidence of Other Crimes Committed by the Accused

At the trial of a person for one crime, the general rule is that the prosecution cannot offer evidence that the defendant committed other offenses. The reason for this rule is the fear that if the jury, or even a judge hearing the case without a jury, learns that the defendant is a law breaker, an inference might thereby arise that he must have committed the offense for which he is now on trial. This, obviously, would be an unfair and risky inference. But the rule has several exceptions.

One exception is where the defendant himself introduces evidence of his good character to show that he is not the kind of man who would do the thing for which he is now accused. By doing this he "opens up the door" for the prosecution to offer evidence of bad character. The showing is made by producing witnesses from the community in which he lives to testify to his reputation with regard to the kind of conduct involved in the particular case. Some courts will permit the reputation to be established from witnesses associated with him in his business, work or other activity.

Another exception occurs when the defendant takes the witness stand to testify in his own behalf. This will allow the prosecution to attack his credibility (that is, impeach him) by cross-examining him regarding prior convictions for offenses that are relevant to the issue of his proneness to lie.

An additional and important exception pertains to other offenses which may explain the intent, motive, or lack of mistake, or which tend to show a common scheme or plan with regard to the offense for which he is now accused. In other words, where such factors are

78

not readily apparent from the particular act itself, other criminal conduct may be considered for the purpose of explaining the one in question.

Example

Frank is prosecuted for a car theft. He claims that he merely drove it away for a "joy ride". The prosecution may refute this defense by proving that Frank had previously been convicted as a car thief.

Example

Jayson is apprehended while entering another person's home. He is charged with attempted burglary and he defends himself by saying he mistook the home to be that of a friend of his whom he went to see, or whose premises he had to enter. The prosecution may offer evidence of Jayson's prior conviction as a burglar.

Example

Huxton is on trial for assaulting Fox. The fact that Huxton had stolen Fox's car on a previous occasion and that Fox had him prosecuted for it would be admissible to show Huxton's motive for assaulting Fox.

Example

Filmore and Weston are charged with conspiracy to rob a bank. The prosecution may show that Filmore stole an automobile to be used as a getaway car, or that Weston slugged and knocked out a bank guard, who was on his way to work, in order to use the guard's uniform. Both are examples of a common scheme or plan.

Proof of Corpus Delicti

The "corpus delicti" rule is one which requires proof of the "body of the crime". In homicide cases, therefore, there can be no conviction unless the prosecution proves that the alleged victim is indeed dead. This rule, as applied to homicide cases, originated out of a concern, all too often substantiated in early days, that, without proof of death, a person caught in a web of circumstantial evidence might be convicted of murdering someone who is still alive.

Example

Mr. and Mrs. Wolfson have been involved in heated quarrels because of his admitted interest in another woman. On several occasions, Mr. Wolfson was heard to say that he wished he could get rid of his wife by any means possible, since she consistently refused to give him a divorce.

One week-end the Wolfsons go to their summer cabin on a steep seaside cliff in a sparsely populated area. Prior to leaving, Wolfson was known to have made a phone call to his girl friend and he was overheard to say, "I love you and hope we can go on a long trip soon. I'll call you Monday about possible details."

On Monday morning Wolfson calls the sheriff and reports that his wife is missing. He says she must have left sometime during the night, and he has no idea what happened to her.

Several months go by without any trace of Mrs. Wolfson, even though the area around the cabin was thoroughly searched and the sea explored for a possible body. Meanwhile, Wolfson went on an extended trip with his girl friend.

A prosecution of Wolfson for the killing of his wife would fail because of lack of proof of death (corpus delicti).

Although in one state (Texas) there can be no homicide prosecution without *direct* proof of the fact of death (that is, some competent witness must testify that he actually saw the dead body, or portions of it), the general rule is that the corpus delicti *can* be proved by *circumstantial* evidence.

Example

In the foregoing case of the Wolfsons, add the following facts. On Sunday night a scream was heard coming from the cabin area. Some traces of blood are found on the cabin floor, in the living room, bedroom, and kitchen, as well as on the steps of the cabin. Although Wolfson said this was the result of a nose bleed he had experienced on Saturday night, scientific tests disclosed that it was of a different blood group from his but the same as his wife's. According to Mrs. Wolfson's sister, there was missing from the cabin a sharp hunting knife which Wolfson kept there. Wolfson denied he ever owned one.

Upon these additional facts, a judge or jury may reasonably conclude that the corpus delicti was established; in other words that Mrs. Wolfson is in fact dead. The conclusion might also be sustained that Wolfson killed her and threw her body into the sea.

Example

Robert and his business partner have had considerable differences over the management of their failing business. One Saturday they are in Robert's cabin cruiser alone. When in the Gulf stream off the Florida keys, the captain of a cruise ship a long way off observes Robert's boat through powerful binoculars. He sees one man hit the other over the head with some object, after which that individual was pushed overboard. The police are alerted by radio. When Robert's boat is docked, he announces that his partner fell overboard and drowned. The police arrest Robert. Police laboratory technicians examine the deck of the boat and find evidence of human blood in the area where the binocular observer said the incident occurred.

Even though the body is never recovered, Robert can be prosecuted for murder. The circumstances clearly establish the partner's death.

Contrary to popular belief, proof of corpus delicti is required in all criminal cases, not just in homicide prosecutions.

Example

Workman is employed by the Ace Company as a truck driver. One night he is seen on the company property pouring gasoline from a large can into his own private automobile tank. This occurs in the vicinity of the pump which is used to supply the company trucks with gasoline. Workman is apprehended and charged with theft of the company's gasoline. He explained to the police that (a) the can was his own (and indeed it was); (b) that he came back that night to get a coat he forgot to take with him when he quit work that day; (c) that he noticed his car tank was dry; and that (d) he removed the can of gas from his car trunk and poured its contents into the tank.

The prosecution would fail unless someone saw Workman take the gas from the company pump, or unless a fingerprint of his was on the pump (and he had no authority to use it), or unless the gas itself could be identified, from its color as company gas.

Section 18

Privileged Communications

THE ATTORNEY-CLIENT PRIVILEGE

The confidential communications of a client to his attorney are privileged from being used in a trial unless the client consents. This privilege, which may stand in the way of the judicial system's search for the truth, is based upon the public policy of encouraging a client to talk to his attorney without fear of having his secret communications subject to subsequent disclosure.

The requirements for the rule to operate include, first, that the client believes he is talking to an attorney in his professional capacity, and second, that the communication must be confidential and made under circumstances reasonably indicating an interest in secrecy. All that is necessary, however, is that the client believes he is talking to an attorney; if this is so, he is entitled to the privilege even though the attorney is actually an impostor or not legally qualified to function as an attorney. However, in any kind of attorney-client relationship, if other persons are present during the conversation, the privilege is lost unless it can be shown that they knew of the confidence and were part of it.

The privilege belongs to the client. It is not the privilege of the lawyer. Only the client, therefore, can waive the privilege and permit the conversation to be disclosed. The privilege survives the death of the client. This is an aspect of the privilege designed to further encourage frank conversations but, understandably, there is an exception in cases involving will contests. Thus, an attorney may testify to what his deceased client said to him regarding the disposition of his property.

The privilege extends not only to spoken words, but also to written communications as well.

In addition to protecting direct communications between a client and his lawyer, the privilege covers what is known as the attorney's "work product"; that is, things he does in preparation for trial, including consultations with other persons, or scientific tests concerned with the case that he may have had made.

There are several exceptions to the attorney-client privilege— situations where it does not apply. It is not applicable to conceal the identity of the client or the fact of employment of the attorney. It also is inapplicable when joint parties later split up and become hostile or sue each other.

For understandable reasons, an attorney who finds it necessary to sue to collect his fee, or to clear his reputation, may make certain disclosures which otherwise would be protected. Likewise, the privilege is not available to conceal consultations made in furtherance of a tort, fraud or other crime. In such instances, considerations of public welfare and safety override the policy in support of the privilege.

The privilege is generally asserted by the client, whether or not he is a party to the lawsuit in which the issue arises. However, an attorney may assert the privilege as agent for the client. In some instances the judge will invoke the privilege on behalf of the client.

The client can waive the privilege, either formally or informally; for example, by not asserting it at a trial where he is present, or by making the communication public himself.

Example

Williams is at a cocktail party and gets into conversation with a casual stranger. Williams asks the stranger what he does for a living and receives the reply "I am an attorney". Williams says "Do you know what? I've been cheating on my taxes for the past 10 years". Assuming that Williams is not attempting to retain his new acquaintance to represent him, he would not be protected by the attorney-client privilege.

Example

Jackson goes to an attorney and says "I want to retain you. Please research all of the cases in which men have been acquitted of killing their wives and then develop me a foolproof legal plan to kill mine". This communication would not be privileged because Jackson consulted the attorney in order to plan a crime.

THE PHYSICIAN-PATIENT PRIVILEGE

The physician-patient privilege excludes from use at trial any confidential communication made by a patient to an examining or prescribing physician. The purpose of this rule is to encourage the patient to make a full disclosure of his ailment to the doctor without fear that what is said may later on be aired in court. The rule, therefore, is designed to promote the health of the patient even at the expense of concealing the truth in the courtroom.

For the rule to operate, there needs to be a *confidential communication* to the doctor out of the presence of other persons whose presence is unnecessary for examination and treatment.

The submission of the patient to an examination by the doctor is considered to be a "communication". In addition to the secrecy of the communication, it is required that the patient be visiting the doctor for the purpose of diagnosis and treatment. However, the privilege does not extend to consultations for an illegal purpose. So if Mrs. Smith went to see a doctor concerning an illegal abortion, nothing about the matter would be privileged.

The privilege belongs to the patient, not the physician. The patient, and only the patient, is accorded the privilege of disclosure or non-disclosure.

The privilege continues after death of the patient, but in certain case situations it can be waived by an heir or next of kin.

The exceptions to this privilege are substantially greater than the other privileges, thus allowing the courts more often to force divulgence of the communications between patient and physician. The privilege does not extend to an action for personal injuries. Thus if Mrs. Smith were to sue a person who has assaulted her, her treating doctor could be compelled to describe the extent of the injuries she sustained. Nor is the privilege applicable in criminal proceedings. Other exclusions include workman's compensation, malpractice, and will-contest actions. Investigations of hospitals and other clinics to improve medical care probably would be excluded also, since the rule is designed primarily to promote health care.

Example
>   Hood goes to a surgeon and inquires as to the possibility of removing skin from his fingertips in order to prevent the taking of his fingerprints for identification purposes. Hood

could not prevent the use of the surgeon's testimony about this visit.

In addition to the general rules with respect to the exceptions and limitations upon the physician-patient privilege, there are various legislative provisions which require physicians to disclose certain information even though it involves someone who comes to them for diagnosis and treatment. Many obligations are imposed for the reporting to governmental agencies of shooting cases, venereal disease cases, etc., accompanied by the name of the patient.

Example
    Byron limps into a doctor's office for the treatment of a bullet wound in his leg. By law the doctor is required to report the case to the police department, despite the fact that Byron came to the doctor as a patient.

THE MARITAL PRIVILEGE

Communications between a wife and husband will generally not be allowed into evidence at a trial.

Some of the protective rules previously discussed (for example, the hearsay rule) are designed to keep out of the trial evidence which may be of questionable truthfulness. On the other hand, the privilege against using conversations between married persons is based upon the public policy of preserving marital confidences and thereby cultivating harmony and frankness between the spouses. While public policy may clearly encourage the solution of crime, the law places the confidential communications of the married couple above this general policy. In a nutshell, the rule is that neither the husband nor the wife may be compelled to testify as to *confidential communications* made by one to the other during their marriage.

The precise rule varies from state to state, depending upon the exact wording of the applicable statute, but generally protection is given to what is described as *private communications.*

Several points can be noted in order to understand the rule. "Private communication" means that the person speaking is not knowingly making a statement for anyone's ears other than those of the spouse. If a third party or a child who is old enough to understand is present, the communication is not privileged. "Communications", in a majority of states, includes not only spoken words, but also acts such as hand gestures, etc. The word "acts" has caused some concern to the courts, but generally it is interpreted to mean something done, which, if disclosed, would weaken the marriage confidence. Such acts, therefore, are privileged.

For the rule to operate, the husband and wife must be married, although common law marriages are included. They must also be living together as a family unit at the time of the communication in question.

Communications made prior to a marriage, or after a divorce, or during a hostile separation, are not privileged.

The privilege also protects communications that were made during the marriage but which are not sought to be divulged until after the death of one of the parties. In other words, the privilege survives after death.

The privilege belongs to the communicating spouse. Put another way, the person who chooses to say something to a spouse, and where to say it, has the right to prevent its disclosure at a trial.

As with most rules, there are several exceptions. The privilege is not applicable in the following classes of lawsuits: an action in which one spouse is charged with a crime against the other spouse, or the children of either; a civil action in which a third party is sued for interfering with the family unit; an action where one spouse sues the other; in some criminal actions where the communication will benefit the spouse-defendant; and in a prosecution for violation of the Mann Act (the federal law prohibiting the transportation of females across state lines for prostitution and "other immoral purposes").

The marital communication privilege should be distinguished from the *competency* of either spouse to testify against the other. Although at one time neither could testify against, *or even for*, each other—on the theory that they were in effect an inseparable unity (e.g., wife belonged to the husband; upon marriage much of her property and wealth became his)—this inhibition has been removed in most states. This means, then, that if a wife sees her husband with a murder victim prior to the killing, or if she happens to see her husband do the killing, she can testify to those observations since there was, in such instances, no "communication" between husband and wife. Similarly, if the wife is aware of evidence helpful to her husband (e.g., an alibi), she can testify for him.

Example

Mr. and Mrs. Foster are married. One evening Mrs. Foster overhears her husband talking on the phone to an unidentified party. She hears him say: "All right, we'll have to get rid of Wilson. Bring him out to the old limestone quarry, and we'll do it there."

Mr. Foster goes out. Two hours later he returns home with bloodstains and grey dust on his shoes. He tells his wife "If anyone asks you; I was home tonight", and he goes upstairs. Later he comes downstairs and tells Mrs. Foster, "You've got a big mouth; this is what you're going to get if you ever *do* talk about my going out tonight". He then hits her, breaking her jaw, to illustrate what he meant.

Upon Foster's trial for the murder of Wilson, Mrs. Foster would not be able to testify about Foster's statements to her that "If anyone asks you, I was home tonight", and "You've got a big mouth. This is what you're going to get if you ever *do* talk about my going out tonight". Both of these statements were direct communications to her by her husband.

However, Mrs. Foster could testify about the telephone conversation she overheard, because this was not a communication to her. She could testify that Foster had blood on his trousers and grey dust on his shoes because this testimony would merely relate to her observations of him; in other words, they were not communications to her.

Example

Foster is being tried for the assault of Mrs. Foster, as described above. Mrs. Foster could testify to Foster's statement, "You've got a big mouth; this is what you're going to get if you ever *do* talk about my going out tonight". The reason for this is that although Foster's statement was a communication made during marriage, an exception exists for communication made in connection with a crime by one spouse against the other.

Example

Mr. and Mrs. Jensen are married. One night Jensen comes home and tells his wife, "I shot Smith and threw his body in the lake". Six months later Mrs. Jensen divorces Jensen. After the divorce Mr. Jensen goes to his wife and tells her, "Don't you ever tell anyone that I told you that I shot Smith and threw his body in the lake". At Jensen's trial for the murder of Smith, the first statement made to his wife, while they were married, would be privileged, and he could prevent his ex-wife from testifying about it. But the second statement, made to Mrs. Jensen after the divorce, would not be privileged and the former Mrs. Jensen could testify about it.

Example

Assume the same facts as in the preceding example, except that right after Jensen first told Mrs. Jensen that he had shot Smith, Mrs. Jensen called the police and told them what Jensen had said. At this point, of course, based on the wife's statement, the police could go and recover Smith's body, arrest Jensen, interrogate him about the murder and, during interrogation, confront him with what his wife had told them. The point to be made here is that just because Mrs. Jensen could not testify at Jensen's trial about a confidential statement made to her during marriage, there is no similar restriction on the police. They may take action on what she told them to any extent they feel to be necessary.

THE ACCOUNTANT-CLIENT PRIVILEGE

In a small number of states a privilege exists as to the confidential communications between an accountant and his client. This privilege belongs to the client. Also, as with other privileges, it does not apply to nonconfidential conversations, such as those conducted in the presence of a third person. The privilege as to confidential communications made during the professional relationship exists even after the accountant has been discharged.

THE MINISTER-PENITENT PRIVILEGE

In many states, a minister, priest, rabbi or other bona fide spiritual advisor cannot testify without the consent of the person making it as to any confidential communication made to him in his professional capacity. The communication, however, must be of the type necessary according to the tenets of the particular sect.

Where the communication is not made in confidence, such as in the presence of a third party, the privilege is not available. Also, where the communication is made to the spiritual leader in a non-ecclesiastical capacity (*i.e.*, a marriage counselor, social worker, or simply as a friend), the privilege does not apply. Moreover, the privilege does not apply to the personal observations of the spiritual leader, even those made during the course of a privileged conversation.

THE NEWS MEDIA PRIVILEGE

In a very few jurisdictions the source of a newspaper reporter's (or radio or television newsman's) information is privileged. The privilege in these states belongs to the newsman, not the informer, and only the newsman can assent to or waive it.

THE ACCIDENT REPORT PRIVILEGE

In most jurisdictions statutes provide a privilege as to the contents of reports required by law to be made and filed with the state by persons involved in automobile accidents. The reason for this privilege is the desire to encourage accurate reporting of accidents as a means of reducing traffic injuries. Although the report filed with the state is privileged, the very same information if communicated to an investigating police officer is not so privileged.

THE INFORMANT PRIVILEGE

As every police officer knows, information from informants is indispensable to effective law enforcement. Whether the informants are paid members of the underworld, police "buffs", or just ordinary citizens, they are the life blood of law enforcement, particularly in clandestine crimes involving narcotics, gambling and stolen property operations. The recent wave of terrorist activities, exemplified by bombings and attacks on police officers, is a new type of guerrilla warfare in which, because of the covert nature of the conspiracies, the use of informants is a vital part of the response.

Confidentiality between a law enforcement officer and his informant is essential to obtaining this type of information. Once the confidentiality ceases the information ceases sometimes by reason of the death or injury of the informant at the hands of those against whom he informed. This also results in a natural reluctance on the part of other potential informants to supply information.

It is for these very reasons that an informant privilege came into being—the general right of the police to refuse to divulge the identity of informants.

Example

Silvertongue, a dope addict, tells officer Stauffer that he heard another dope addict say that Smith killed Jones during a burglary. Following that tip, the police locate a witness who saw Smith pawn some jewelry the day after Jones was killed. The jewelry is identified as having belonged to Jones.

When confronted with the pawned jewelry evidence, Smith confesses. At Smith's trial he has no right to a disclosure of how the police got a line on him.

The only time the identity of a police informant need be disclosed is when the informant actually participated in the crime for which the defendant is charged, or when the disclosure of the informant's identity would "materially aid" the defense. Even then, of course, one way to continue to preserve the confidentiality and to protect the informant is to dismiss the charge against the defendant and thereby abandon the prosecution. There may be some occasions when this will have to be done.

Example

Drug addict Walton, a reliable informant, tells the police that Druggist Jones is selling narcotics without the required physician's prescription. Walton is supplied with marked money to make a purchase, and before he goes into the store he is thoroughly searched to be sure he does not already have narcotics in his possession.

An exchange transaction between Jones and Walton is observed by a detective in the store. He immediately arrests Jones, recovers the marked money, and then obtains the narcotics from Walton.

Since the informant was a participant in the transaction, his identity must be disclosed to the accused and an opportunity accorded the defense to interview him or to have him produced as a witness. This disclosure might be of "material aid" in support of a contention that the defendant was "entrapped" or even framed with a completely false charge.

Most courts (a notable exception being the California Supreme Court) have rather narrowly interpreted the meaning of the "material aid" requirement for informant identity disclosure. The courts insist upon a clear showing of need and will not be satisfied with vague allegations of the defendant's attorney. For sound public policy reasons they are reluctant to permit the defendant to go on a "fishing expedition" to secure the identity of the informant.

Although nondisclosure of the identity of the informant is the general rule, subject to the two above noted exceptions, there are certain conditions regarding informants which must be established in order for the prosecution to support the probable cause required for a search based upon informant information. Either one or the other of the following elements must be proved:

1. The informant had previously given information about criminal activities which proved to be true, and, in the present case, the informant was specific as to the basis for the information he revealed.

2. The information received from an informant, whether previously established as reliable or not, was checked out by the police and a reasonable amount of substantiation resulted therefrom.

Example

Officer Stoll receives a tip that Phillips is peddling dope. The tip came from Bates whom Stoll had just seen for the first time as he was being arrested for public intoxication. Stoll arrests Phillips and finds heroin in his pockets.

The evidence will be suppressed because there was a lack of probable cause (reasonable grounds) for the arrest.

Example

Officer Remington of the narcotics squad is told by dope addict Graves that Jones is a peddler of narcotics; that Graves saw Jones make three sales on the street that very day. On two previous occasions Graves had given Remington information that had proved to be accurate and had resulted in the apprehension of four possessors of narcotics.

Acting upon this information, Remington arrests Jones at a street corner, and a search of his pockets produces heroin.

Remington acted upon probable cause, the heroin evidence is usable against Jones and Graves's identity need not be disclosed.

Example

Officer Harley is told by Carter, a pickpocket, that Young sells heroin at the corner of First and Main Street. Harley, in civilian dress, goes there and, from a roof top, he observes persons approach Young on six different occasions. Each time Young and the other person would go into an alley where something would be handed to Young who, in turn, would hand something to the other person. Harley then goes to the corner, arrests Young and finds heroin in his possession.

Harley's actions were based upon probable cause and the evidence is admissible.

(Where the evidence sought is located in a home or place of business, a search warrant could be issued upon the basis of information similar to that in the two preceding examples.)

Competency to Stand Trial
and the Insanity Defense

Regardless of an accused person's mental condition at the time of the commission of the act for which he is being prosecuted, the trial cannot begin or continue if he is mentally *incompetent* at that time. The criteria for determining incompetency to stand trial is entirely different, however, from the criteria for determining whether a person was legally *insane* at the time of the commission of the act for which he is on trial.

INCOMPETENCY

Before a person can be tried for a criminal offense he must understand the nature and object of the proceedings and to be able to confer with his lawyer with a reasonable degree of rational understanding. If he lacks the ability to do this, the prosecution will have to be postponed until he develops that capacity. Meanwhile, he will be committed to a mental institution. Where the capacity is never achieved, he may remain in the mental institution for the rest of his life—not as a criminal, but as a mentally ill person for whom institutional confinement is required for his own welfare as well as the welfare of the public.

Example
    Edwards is a farmer who lived alone for many years. He butchered his own cattle in his barn for what meat he himself needed. One day, however, it was found out that he had also butchered several women in the same way as he did his cattle. Upon his arrest Ed "looked crazy" and a psychiatric

examination confirmed that he did not understand what the arrest and the charge of murder were "all about".

Edwards must be committed to a mental institution until such time as he knows what the trial is "all about" and he is able to confer adequately with his lawyer regarding the matter.

INSANITY

No one can be held legally accountable for an act which he commits while insane. To do so would be in violation of the constitutional guarantee that no person can be deprived of his life, liberty, or property without "due process of law".

One of the earliest and most widely adopted tests of insanity was the one which states that no one can be held accountable for an act if at the time of its commission—and due to a *diseased mind*—he did not know "right from wrong". It is referred to as either the *right-wrong test* or as the *M'Naghten test*. M'Naghten was the name of the defendant in the early English case in which the right-wrong test was first applied.

Although for many years practically all of the state courts, and the federal courts as well, adhered to the right-wrong test, it was ultimately supplemented in many courts by the *irresistible impulse test*. According to this one, even though a person knew right from wrong he could not be held criminally responsible if, because of a disease of the mind, he acted upon an impulse which it was impossible for him to control.

In recent years two other tests were developed and accepted by some courts. One was the *Durham test* which was adopted by the Court of Appeals for the District of Columbia. According to it, a person could not be held criminally responsible if his act was the *product* of a mental disease or defect. Another test is one which holds that there can be no criminal responsibility on the part of a person who, because of a mental disease or defect, lacks *substantial capacity* either to appreciate the criminality of his conduct or conform his conduct to the requirements of the law. This is the most popular test today, and the one that is gaining more and more acceptance. It is known as the *A. L. I. test* because it was formulated by the American Law Institute.

A person who is found insane by any of the foregoing tests will be acquitted of the offense charged against him. However, if mental examinations conducted after his acquittal establish that he should be placed in a mental institution for care and treatment he may be thus committed in a civil proceeding.

Evidence of insanity may be in the form of either lay witness testimony or the testimony of psychiatrists, or both.

Example

Ewald is accused of murdering Cox. Ewald's relative Smith may testify that when Ewald was a young boy he fell down a pit and was unconscious for several hours; that ever since the fall he has acted strangely; that he did a lot of "crazy things"; and that he never seemed to know right from wrong.

Example

In the foregoing case of Ewald, a psychiatrist conducts a mental examination and from that examination he concludes that at the time of the act in question Ewald did not know right from wrong or, depending upon the particular court test, that his act was the product of a disease or defect of mind, or that he lacked substantial capacity to measure up to the requirements of the law; and that, therefore, he was legally insane.

In all cases involving capacity to stand trial or the issue of insanity at the time of the act, it is up to the jury (or a judge in a non-jury case) to ultimately make that determination.

Although laymen ordinarily read or hear about the defenses of mental incapacity or insanity in homicide cases, the two defenses are available in any kind of criminal prosecution.

In addition to the foregoing mental condition case situations, mention must be made of one other—the case of the person who, after conviction, becomes insane. To him there is also given special consideration. For instance, even though a person may have had the capacity to stand trial on a murder charge, and even though he was sane at the time of the killing as well as at the time the court sentenced him to death, he cannot be executed if he subsequently becomes insane. Some jurisdictions have this rule by statutory law; others have it by court decision law. In either situation the basic reason is that no one should be executed unless he understands the "nature and purpose" of the sentence of death. An auxiliary reason is that a person should always be given an opportunity to "make peace with God", which, so the reasoning goes, an insane person is unable to do. Then, too, there is the argument that a person awaiting execution may be able to come up with something to establish his innocence or a justification for a commutation of the death sentence—an opportunity that does not exist in the case of an insane person.

The Investigator's Role
in Securing Evidence

A very important practical investigative guideline that should be followed by all investigators is that the proof of guilt that may satisfy an investigator may be insufficient to convince a jury composed of laymen inexperienced and untrained as evidence evaluators. What may be convincing incriminating evidence to the investigator may be only a suspicious circumstance to the factory worker, housewife, sales clerk, or even the business or professional man sitting on a jury. Moreover, his judgment is not merely affected by inexperience and lack of training; he may also have been conditioned to a defense-oriented viewpoint by the fiction he has read or seen portrayed on the movie or television screen. Then, as a climax, he is told by the judge that the law requires the prosecution to prove the defendant's guilt *"beyond a reasonable doubt"*.

It is vitally necessary, therefore, that the investigator look for—and properly preserve—far more incriminating evidence than that which has already convinced him of the suspect's guilt. (Guidelines for the proper preservation of evidence of a scientific nature are presented in another book in the Inbau Law Enforcement Series—*Scientific Police Investigation.*)

EVIDENCE FAVORABLE TO THE DEFENSE

Fairness requires that there be no concealment of evidence favorable to the defense. It is also a principle that has been given binding legal effect by the Supreme Court of the United States.

98

It is not enough that there be no concealment of such evidence—the Supreme Court has also decreed that the prosecution turn the evidence over to defense counsel.

Whenever, therefore, an investigating officer or any officer learns of evidence favorable to the accused he is morally as well as legally bound to tell the prosecuting attorney about it. It then becomes the duty of the prosecution to make a disclosure of it to the lawyer for the defendant.

Example

Officer Harmon investigates a murder and develops considerable evidence that the victim was killed by Royce acting alone. However, Harmon did learn that Gordon was seen near the scene at the time of the murder.

Even though Officer Harmon is thoroughly convinced of Royce's guilt, and that Gordon was in no way implicated, Harmon must disclose to the prosecutor what he learned about Gordon's presence. Then the prosecutor must make a disclosure to defense counsel.

Example

Officer Ingram, assigned to the case of the rape of Louise H., develops excellent evidence of Nance's guilt. He did learn, though, that Sadie, a prostitute, told another officer that Nance was with her at the time Louise was raped. From his experience Ingram is convinced that Sadie is a liar, but he must disclose what he learned about her to the prosecutor who, in turn, must make a disclosure to defense counsel.

In certain types of cases, the defense must make certain disclosures to the prosecution. A number of states, by legislative action, require that whenever the defense will be that of alibi, the prosecution must be so advised in advance of trial. Some statutes further require a disclosure of the details of the alibi (i.e., names and addresses of witnesses). A failure to make the required disclosures will prevent the use of alibi witnesses, except where the alibi information did not come to defense counsel until the time of trial.

Similarly, some states, by statute, require that if the defense is to be based upon the insanity of the accused, that fact must be made known to the prosecutor in advance of trial.

Perhaps a good rule of thumb to follow is for the investigator to ask himself this question: "If I were an ordinary layman, without the savvy of a police officer in matters of this sort, would the evidence I have obtained thus far convince me of this person's guilt beyond a reasonable doubt?" If an objective answer is "perhaps not", he should continue his efforts to secure whatever additional evidence there may be.

The Police Officer
as a Courtroom Witness[*]

Top flight police work—whether the result of a carefully planned and thorough investigation, a spectacular arrest or an effective interrogation—may be completely nullified by a few mistakes in the preparation of the case for trial or by a poor performance of the investigator on the witness stand. It is highly essential, therefore, that the investigation be climaxed with a proper and persuasive presentation of the evidence of guilt.

TRIAL PREPARATION

Trial preparation actually begins at the start of the investigation in those instances where the investigator's efforts are likely to result in a criminal trial. Of utmost importance is *accuracy in all report writing*. Inaccuracy in police reports can, and frequently does, seriously damage the prosecution's case, and is accompanied, sometimes, by considerable embarrassment to the officer-witness, or indeed to other witnesses who would be adversely affected by an inaccurate report. The damage and embarrassment occur when defense counsel cross-examines and seeks to impeach a witness by confronting him with the inaccuracies in the police report.

Example
> Mrs. Winslow told Officer Walsh that the man who robbed her was fairly tall. Walsh, a large man himself, writes in his report that she said the robber was over 6 feet. On the witness stand, Mrs. Winslow, a woman about 5 feet 4 inches in height, says the man was about 5 feet 7 inches tall. On cross-

[*] For his suggestions regarding the present subject and the following one, we are deeply indebted to Mr. William J. Martin of the Chicago Bar.

101

examination she is asked if it is not a fact that she told the
police the man was 6 feet tall. She denies this and states that
she merely said he was "tall". To her 5 feet 7 inches is tall; to
the officer one must be at least 6 feet before he can be described as "tall."

In such instances the witness is embarrassed, and the prosecutor's case weakened, both of which situations could have
been avoided by accurate reporting.

Before writing a report of what a witness said, the officer-inves-
tigator should be sure he clearly understands what the witness did
in fact say. Then an accurate recording of it should be made.

With respect to descriptions of an offender, no suggestions should
be made as to specifics; to put words into the witness's mouth may
have a choking effect later in the courtroom.

Rather than suggest or insist that a witness give a specific height,
weight, complexion and other data regarding the offender, it is better
to let him give a description in fairly general terms—for example,
"tall", "short", "heavyset", "light to medium complexion", or perhaps
better yet, the witness may be asked to compare the offender with
his brother, father, or even someone else present at the interview.
Then the witness and the investigator will be able to come up with
a fairly accurate approximation in terms of feet and inches, pounds,
complexion, etc. Even then, in recognition of the fallibility of witness identifications, the witness should be allowed some flexibility,
such as between 5 feet 6 inches and 5 feet 8 inches, or between 150
and 170 pounds.

It is the same with distances, as in an automobile accident case.
Rather than ask a witness to state how far the pedestrian was from
the curb when he was hit, let the witness point out, preferably at
the scene itself if possible, about how far away the victim was.
Thereafter the pointed-out distance itself can be measured, and
noted by the witness. Then when the witness testifies in court, he
will be able to say, with far greater accuracy, what the approximate
distance was in terms of feet.

Prior to the time of trial the investigating officer should refresh
his recollection of case details by a careful reading of all the reports
in the police file, his own as well as those of fellow officers. This
also holds true with respect to the recorded testimony presented at
coroner's inquests and grand jury hearings. Then, too, either he or

the prosecutor should be sure to allow prospective witnesses to refresh their recollection by examining whatever statements they
signed or whatever records there are of what the witnesses are supposed to have said previously.

In some instances the investigating officer will find it helpful to
visit the crime scene. By doing so he may avoid erroneous descrip-
tive details during his testimony, and particularly while on cross-examination. The lapse of time between the investigation and the
trial, and the investigations of intervening cases frequently dull the
memory of any given case. By these various processes the conse-
quent effect may be diminished and more accurate and persuasive
testimony will be forthcoming at the trial.

Competent prosecutors will attempt to confer in advance of trial,
or certainly prior to the call to the witness stand, with the persons
he expects to call as witnesses, including the police officers themselves. This procedure is a practical necessity and is thoroughly eth-
ical and legally permissible. It is also proper for a prospective officer-witness to discuss the case and any aspect of it with fellow
investigating officers.

If, while under cross-examination by defense counsel, the officer-
witness is asked whether prior to coming to court, or while in court,
he discussed the case with the prosecutor or with other officers, the
answer should be an unhesitating "yes".

Sometimes defense counsel, discontent with such a truthful answer, will then inquire, "Didn't the prosecutor (or your command-
ing officer, or someone else) tell you what to say?", in which event
no hesitation should be encountered in truthfully responding with a
"no", or, where it can be truthfully said, the answer may be, "He
told me to relate the facts as I know them to be; in other words, tell
the truth."

Some officer-witnesses have sustained a terrible embarrassment,
or even seriously damaged the prosecutor's case, by being unwill-
ing, or even merely being hesitant, to admit to a pre-trial conference or discussion about the case. Sensing a dishonest answer, the
judge or jury might discount all of the officer's testimony, despite
its absolute truthfulness.

A prosecutor will acquaint a novice police officer witness with
the procedures he will use in getting physical objects and documents into evidence. They must be marked as exhibits, and in testi-

fying about them the officer witness should refer to them by their identification mark (e.g., State's Exhibit #5) as he testifies about them.

As a matter of fact, during the pretrial conference with an inexperienced police officer-witness, the prosecutor should brief him about all of the essential features of the officer's courtroom experience.

PHYSICAL APPEARANCE AND GENERAL CONDUCT OF THE OFFICER-WITNESS

Perhaps the best single piece of advice which can be offered to a prospective police officer-witness is this: *You are a professional; look and act like one!* An officer's professional looking appearance and conduct will render his courtroom testimony more effective, and also reflect credit upon his department and upon the police profession generally.

Where circumstances render it unavoidable that the officer-witness come to court in uniform, the uniform should be clean and his entire appearance neat. Where the preferred civilian dress is feasible the officer should wear a suit, or sports coat, with necktie. Of course, no officer should ever take the witness stand with gum, tobacco, or any other such substance in his mouth.

While on the stand the officer-witness should sit erect and speak loudly enough for the juror farthest away to hear him. When speaking he should look in the general direction of the jury box, unless he is responding to a question from the judge.

During the direct examination of the officer-witness, the prosecutor may ask him to testify in narrative terms, or he may be asked specific questions. For the narration the question may be: "Officer, will you please tell us what you observed when you came upon the scene?" Specific questions may be such as: "Whom did you see when you arrived?"; "What time was it when you got there?"; "Who was with you when you received the call to go to the scene?" The form used will be determined by the particular nature of the case or the prosecutor's discretion as to the most effective course to follow.

When specific questions are employed the witness should respond only to that question; he should not volunteer anything else. Particular care should be taken to avoid any unsolicited information about a defendant's prior criminal record, either conviction or mere arrest. Anything of that sort can result in a mistrial or reversal on appeal.

In his testimony the officer-witness should avoid the use of words and expressions that are not in common usage by ordinary citizens; or, stated another way, he should stand clear of "law enforcement lingo". Here is what we mean, although the illustration itself may be in slightly exaggerated form.

Example

Officer Roberts is testifying about a raid in a narcotics case. He said: "We got a squeal from one of our regulars that the offender in this case was holding smack at his pad at 641 Main Street. We staked it out and saw two hippies that we'd busted go in."

Such language would be comprehensible to most experienced narcotics officers, but not to the average judge or juror. The same testimony should be presented somewhat as follows:

We received information from an informant with whom we had dealt in the past that the defendant had a supply of heroin at his apartment at 641 Main Street. We placed that address under surveillance and observed two addicts, whom we had arrested before, go into that address.

When referring to the victim of the crime, his or her last name should be used instead of "the victim". Rather than "apprehend" the defendant, the expression should be "caught" or "arrested"— expressions that mean more to the layman than "apprehend". Also, as indicated above, the defendant should be referred to as such, rather than as "the offender", which implies, of course, that he is guilty, a determination yet to be made in the case by the judge or jury.

When giving the time of an incident or occurrence the officer-witness should not use military/police terminology such as 1305 but rather civilian terminology such as 1:05 P.M.

In answer to a question asked by either the prosecutor or defense counsel the officer-witness should avoid any such prefatory statements as "to tell you the truth" or "to be honest with you . . ." Such statements detract from the persuasiveness of the answer. Obviously, however, if the witness is not sure or does not know what the answer is he should say so. The witness is not expected to know everything about which he is questioned, whether it be departmental practices or policies or information about the particular case in which he is testifying. He should have no reluctance, therefore, to respond at times with the blunt answer of "I don't know". This is far more honest and far less damaging to the prosecutor's case than a halting, equivocal answer that will afford defense counsel an opportunity to descredit all of the witness's testimony by exposing his lack of frankness and honesty in some one answer.

The real test of an officer-witness's capability will come when he is under cross-examination by defense counsel.

All officer-witnesses should recognize that in contrast to their function—the impartial presentation of the facts as they know them to be—defense counsel is expected to perform in a partisan manner. His primary obligation is to his client, and he is duty bound to do the best he can to test out the credibility and the accuracy of the prosecutor's witnesses. Once this function is recognized, officer-witnesses will realize that except for the rarest of cases the issue is not a personalized one; the aim is not to embarrass or ridicule the officer-witness *as a person,* but to disclose the possible weaknesses in his *official function* in the case on trial.

To be sure, some defense counsel take great delight in applying the arts of ridicule and insult in an effort to rattle any prosecutor's witnesses. They know, too, that a rattled witness is apt to be an ineffective witness. The only way to combat such tactics, however, is for the witness to maintain his composure—to "play it cool", so to speak. If he tries to do battle with defense counsel, he will almost always lose, as is expected of a rank amateur boxer pitted against an experienced pro. The attorney knows all the rules of his profession and will generally have experience to draw upon for whatever he attempts to do in his cross-examination.

No sarcasm should be employed toward defense counsel, even when a justifiable impulse exists. For instance, when counsel comes up with repetitious questions the natural impulse is to say "I've already answered that", but it is far better to respond without making any such remark. Then, too, it is better to address the cross-examiner by his name rather than refer to him as "counsel", because it is difficult for an officer-witness to conceal his contempt when he says "counsel", whereas the concealment is easier with the words "Mr. Smith". In addressing the judge, the preferred designation is "Your honor", rather than "judge".

Of all the advice we can offer to the officer-witness, the most important is that he should tell the truth as he testifies. To do otherwise could endanger the life or liberty of an innocent person. Apart from considerations of morality with respect to not telling the truth, there are two additional factors deserving the officer's consideration: the degrading effect upon him personally, and the long range damaging effect upon law enforcement generally.

Other Books in the Inbau Law Enforcement Series

Criminal Law for the Police,
            by Fred E. Inbau and Marvin E. Aspen

Criminal Law for the Layman,
            by Fred E. Inbau and Marvin E. Aspen

Fingerprints and The Law,
            by Andre A. Moenssens

Fingerprint Techniques
            by Andre A. Moenssens

Scientific Police Investigation
            by Fred E. Inbau, Andre A. Moenssens, and
            Louis R. Vitullo

Index